MISREADING
SHAKESPEARE

MISREADING SHAKESPEARE:

Modern Playwrights and the Quest for Originality

WAGDI ZEID

iUniverse, Inc.
Bloomington

MISREADING SHAKESPEARE:
Modern Playwrights and the Quest for Originality

iUniverse books may be ordered through booksellers or by contacting:

iUniverse
1663 Liberty Drive
Bloomington, IN 47403
www.iuniverse.com
1-800-Authors (1-800-288-4677)

ISBN: 978-1-4759-5204-9 (sc)
ISBN: 978-1-4759-5205-6 (hc)
ISBN: 978-1-4759-5206-3 (e)

Library of Congress Control Number: 2012918034

Printed in the United States of America

iUniverse rev. date: 10/05/2012

For Professor Marvin Carlson, the world's leading authority in theatre theory

Contents

FOREWORD   IX

INTRODUCTION   XI

1.   AT THE CROSSROADS   1

2.   BOND VERSUS SHAKESPEARE   15

3.   DISCONTINUITY AND THE DOMINANCE OF ANTITHESIS   25

4.   STOPPARD AND INFLUENCE   43

5.   FOREGROUNDING THE ABSURD   49

ENDNOTES   73

BIBLIOGRAPHY   85

Foreword

This study, an application of Harold Bloom's theories of influence to several important theatre texts, is a stimulating and original piece of work that shows the author's excellent knowledge both of the theatre under examination and of the theoretical position of Bloom and other related theorists.

Dr. Zeid is indeed an exceptional scholar, intelligent and highly motivated, and I am sure his future career will bring honor both to his native country of Egypt and to the City University of New York.

MARVIN CARLSON
DISTINGUISHED PROFESSOR OF THEATRE
CITY UNIVERSITY OF NEW YORK

Introduction

Dramatic criticism has not yet closely examined Harold Bloom's theory of the anxiety of influence. While Bloom has applied his theory to the Romantic poets and the lyric form, neither he nor any other critic has tried to demonstrate how far this theory could operate by applying it to dramatists. Although "it was in the name of drama that the Romantics assailed neoclassicism,"[1] Bloom, by his own admission, excludes not only Shakespeare but all dramatists before and after him, be they Romantics or otherwise, from his theory.

Nevertheless, this takes for granted Bloom's claim that his is a theory of poetry; by definition, then, the theory is applicable to all writers of all literary genres. We shall attempt to see how far Bloom's theory of the anxiety of influence can be applied to the dramatists Edward Bond, Tom Stoppard, and William Shakespeare.

No major attempt has been made so far to concretely define, from a theoretical perspective, the relationship between Shakespeare's *King Lear* and *Hamlet* and Bond and Stoppard's respective versions of these plays, *Lear* and *Rosencrantz and Guildenstern Are Dead*. Previous studies have tended to emphasize thematic similarities and differences but not offered a theory of influence based on concrete analyses of the four plays. Critics acknowledge that Bond's play is dependent on Shakespeare's in a wholly creative sense, and that Stoppard's play, though "recognizably derivative," [2] is genuinely different from Shakespeare's. Yet no critic has provided a theoretical perspective for the relationships between the modern versions and the Shakespearean originals.

Existing studies of Bond's *Lear* and Stoppard's *Rosencrantz and Guildenstern Are Dead* are exclusively concerned either with their contemporary influences or with the original Shakespearean play as a "point of departure"[3]; they seldom explore the intra-dramatic relationship between the modern versions and the originals. In her article "Edward Bond's *Lear*," Leslie Smith, for instance, writes about "Brecht's social and political purposiveness allied to Strindberg's tormented vision of man's self-destructiveness," which constitutes Bond's "double vision."[4] "Bond," she states, "has a great playwright's ability to express this double vision in dramatic images, in dialogue and action that have extraordinary force and power."[5] Regarding the influence of Shakespeare, she merely quotes Bond's words: "I can only say that Lear was standing in my path and I had to get him out of the way. I couldn't get beyond him to do other things that I also wanted, so I had to come to terms with him."[6] Smith does not relate Bond's words to his play to show us why and how Lear was standing in Bond's path, or why and how Bond had to come to terms with Lear. Instead, she simply ends her article with the conclusion that "Bond completes a play ...

which does not suffer by comparison with Shakespeare's great original."[7]

Other academic commentators discuss *Rosencrantz and Guildenstern Are Dead* in a similar manner. For them, Stoppard's play is nothing but a combination of "the brittle wit of Oscar Wilde with mordant humour of Samuel Beckett,"[8] or a "spirited union of materials from various dramatic and nondramatic sources."[9] They describe its composition as if it had been "neatly prescribed by a recipe: plot and character from Shakespeare folded into a Beckettian *ambiance*, or vice versa; a dash of concept, echo or tone from the other dramatic or literary sources; and Wittgenstein's philosophy cracked, its language-games separated and used to bind the other ingredients."[10] However, I agree with Jill Levenson's judgment that Stoppard's play does not resemble the composition of "pudding."[11] Despite the influences we may recognize in it, Stoppard's play offers a vision as harmonious and distinct as that offered by *Hamlet*.

Like these studies, my master's thesis, written and submitted in 1982 to the American University in Cairo, did not include a theoretical perspective. It was a comparative study of *Rosencrantz and Guildenstern Are Dead* and *Hamlet* in which I exclusively examined similarities in dramatic technique and language.

This present study seeks to provide that theoretical perspective with a twofold strategy. It deals with the tradition of influence, showing what debts Bloom owes to his precursors and how his theory can be adapted to the needs of dramatic criticism, and it also tests the theory against the relationship between Bond and Stoppard's plays and the Shakespearean originals.

One aim of this research is to formulate a theoretical perspective by which we can define the relationship between old and new dramatic works. Another aim is to discover how Bloom's theory of the anxiety of influence operates when applied to the dramatists Bond and Stoppard, and to their relationship to William Shakespeare.

This thesis is divided into five chapters. The primary aim of the first chapter is to provide the required theoretical perspective for examining the relationships of the plays. Bloom's concept of influence is considered in relation to the concepts of W. Jackson Bate and T. S. Eliot, his two most important precursors.[12] In light of the conclusions of chapter one, the following four chapters investigate the relationships between Bond, Stoppard, and Shakespeare, and their plays.

CHAPTER ONE

At the Crossroads

Influence, as conceived by Harold Bloom, has a history as old as literary history itself. Tracing it, W. Jackson Bate looks back to "an almost forgotten" Egyptian writer of 2000 BC, Khakheperresenb, "who inherited in his literary legacy no Homer, Sophocles, Dante, Shakespeare, Milton, Goethe, or Dickens—no formidable variety of literary genres available in thousands of libraries—yet who still left the poignant epigram: 'Would I had phrases that are not known, utterances that are strange, in new language that has not been used, free from repetition, not an utterance which has grown stale, which men of old have spoken.'"[1]

Influence as anxiety, or, as Bate puts it, "the remorseless deepening of self-consciousness before the rich and intimidating legacy of the past,"[2] has been felt and indeed acknowledged in all ages. Sixteen centuries ago, in his *On the Sublime*, Longinus wondered "why minds of a high order of sublimity and greatness are no longer produced," and "why this world-wide barrenness of literature ...

1

pervades our life."[3] Ortega y Gasset stated that every age will inevitably feel itself to be empty in comparison with the past. Bate assures us that major writers from the Renaissance to the present day have privately wrestled with this dilemma. The nagging questions that have "haunted every poet since Milton, however much he may have resisted" them, are these: What is there left to write about? How, as craftsmen, do poets find not only new subjects but also a new idiom? Bate points out that the anxiety of influence has become one of the greatest challenges of art, and that it will become increasingly so.[4] Bloom further predicts:

> There is no escape. It is simply the given, and there is nothing we can do. In fact all we can do is keep increasing it, and this of course is where Hegel is the prophet. Hegel prophesied that this must finally mark the death of art, because this growing self-awareness, this growing self-consciousness must finally be destructive of the aesthetic.[5]

- Bate is Bloom's immediate precursor. Indeed, in Bate's book *The Burden of the Past and the English Poet* (1970) we can trace the basic premise of Bloom's theory, which he later proposed in his book *The Anxiety of Influence* (1973). Bloom's argument is based on Bate's successful and bold attempt to pose the problem and bring it out into the open. Bate discusses several diagnoses advanced by major writers of different periods. After each diagnosis, he restates the problem, opening up many different avenues. Bloom's theory, as we will see, is no more than the exploration—if not exhaustion— of one such avenue.

Investigating the diagnoses, Bate finds that most major writers between the Renaissance—the epoch of Shakespeare and Milton—and the Victorian and modern ages (1660–1830) are intimidated by the "brilliantly creative achievement"[6] before them. Dryden, for instanc e, described writers before the Restoration as "the giant race before the flood."[7] Dryden's successor, Alexander Pope, said, "If ever there was any author who deserved the name of an original, it was Shakespeare."[8] Goethe frankly admitted, "Shakespeare has already exhausted the whole of human nature in all directions and in all depths and heights ... For those who came after him, there remains nothing more to do."[9]

Bate also realizes that the views of English writers such as Johnson, Edward Young, and Blake are not practically useful, even though they address the problem of originality in more optimistic terms. Johnson believed that originality is always possible if only we "shed our superstitious reverence of the dead."[10] Similarly, Blake said, "Drive your cart and your plow over the bones of the dead."[11] Young's advice was for the writer to "pull himself up by his own bootstraps" and "imitate the general spirit of the past writers we admire."[12] None of these views, however, tells the writer practically how to achieve the originality attributed to Shakespeare.

Bate's own diagnosis is that we are caught in a self-created prison that we can escape only if we know how to cut down to size the taboo of repetition. He says "the complaint ... that all topics are preoccupied" is repeated only by the timid or the militantly conservative, and is a complaint "by which some discourage others and some themselves."[12] The burden of the past is the burden of choice. The Romantics succeeded because they knew when and how to make their own choices. They were the children of the period that was "beginning to develop antibodies, so to speak,"[14] and learning "to lift the burden of the past or to shift it to one side."[15] The greatest lesson we can learn from them is "the value of boldness."[16] Despite the odds against them, eighteenth-century artists explored the very nature of beauty. This boldness involves

4

"directly facing up to what we admire and then trying to be like it (the old Greek ideal of education, of *paideia*, of trying to be like the excellent, or *arete*, that we have come to admire—whatever our self-defensive protests)."[17]

Bate's conclusion, which later serves as Bloom's point of departure, is that a major achievement of the eighteenth-century Enlightenment was their discovery of how "open and elusive (indeed potentially self-contradictory)" the premise of originality is; for this reason, they created "their own ideal of originality."[18] Bloom showed himself to be the disciple of Bate, the Enlightenment, and the Romantics by taking from them this premise of originality as open, elusive, and potentially self-contradictory; he determined that he could be original as a critic by building his entire theory of influence around "the essence of neurosis": conflict.[19] Bloom himself admits, "insofar as I find a wavering center in my own work, it would be the notion of the *agon*.[20] Indeed, this notion of agon (conflict) is the single most principle we must keep in mind when comparing Bloom's concept of influence to his precursor T. S. Eliot's sense of tradition.

M. H. Abrams claims that Bloom uses the phrase "the anxiety of influence" to identify his "radical revision" of the standard theory that influence is a "direct borrowing, or assimilation, of the materials and features found in earlier writers."[21] Abrams' statement implies that before Bloom, the theory of influence was a one-way system. This implication is, I believe, an oversimplification. Similarly, in recent studies critics have maintained that T. S. Eliot saw tradition as mere repetition. Before we proceed, we must reach a better understanding of Eliot's concept of tradition.

Close study of Eliot's two essays "Tradition and the Individual Talent" and "The Function of Criticism at The Present Time," written more than fifty years before Bloom proposed his theory, reveals that Eliot sees tradition not as a stagnant pool, but as friction or tension between the poet and his predecessors—that is, between the present and the past, between new and old works of art. Indeed, Eliot even warns us against the implications of Abrams and other critics. Eliot states:

> Yet if the only form of tradition, of handing down, consisted in following the ways of the immediate generation before us in a blind or timid adherence to its successes, "tradition" should positively be discouraged.[22]

For Eliot, tradition "is a matter of much wider significance."[23] In his view, a poet does not "inherit" a tradition; he must obtain it through "great labor." The poet must have a historical sense that involves "a perception, not only of the pastness of the past, but of its presence."[24] It is this historical sense that compels the poet "to write not merely with his own generation in his bones, but with a feeling that the whole of the literature of Europe from Homer and within it the whole of the literature of his own country has a simultaneous order."[25] It is "a sense of the timeless as well as of the temporal."[26] Eliot is clearly aware that no poet "has his complete meaning alone." He goes even further to say, "the past should be altered by the present as much as the present is directed by the past."[27] Bloom's seemingly bold notion of the belated poet determining his precursor's law, or the strong poet failing to beget himself and waiting for his son to "define him as he defined his Poetic Father,"[28] echo the first half of Eliot's statement.

In "Tradition and The Individual Talent" and "The Function of Criticism at The Present Time," Eliot offers a theory of poetry whose practical objective is to direct attention to the poetry itself rather than to the poet. He describes this as an "impersonal theory" of poetry in order to distinguish it from Romantic, literary, and philosophical theories. Eliot attacks the importance attached to personality and the shift from the objective outlook of classical times to the subjective outlook of Romanticism. Eliot's theory is impersonal and objective; Romantic theory, is personal and subjective.

The poet, Eliot says, in virtue of acquiring a historical sense, stands in subtle relation to the entire body of poetry before him. His work can only be fully appreciated and understood when he is set within this body of poetry, which Eliot conceives of as "an ideal order," a "principle of aesthetic, not merely historical criticism."[29]

Eliot observes that poetry is not the expression of personal emotion; it is a concentration of impressions and experiences. What the poet has to express is not "a personality," but "a particular medium."[30] It is common practice to value what is individual in a poet's work. But, Eliot says, if we approach a poet without this prejudice, we will find that "not only the best, but the most individual parts of his work may be those in which the dead poets, his ancestors, assert their immortality most vigorously."[31]

Lewis Freed has suggested that Eliot's ideas about tradition and historical sense are developed from the particular way "in which he conceives the relation of the past and the present."[32] He explains that, Eliot's notion of the past is not "the past of archaeology or of philology—a record of objects, events, ideas, institution, or literary monuments classified according to types and periods representing factual knowledge of bygone times."[33] Nor is it "the past which we reconstruct with the help of such knowledge and by an exercise of the historical imagination, projecting ourselves into other periods and re-enacting modes of thought and feeling other than our own."[34] In Eliot's view, there is only one time, which is ever present, for there is no time apart from consciousness, and consciousness is always a present fact. "Past and present are distinctions within time but for the poet they are one."[35] The poet lives in the present, and his awareness of the past is part of his experience, so the past and present exist together in a moment of consciousness. Thus, the past that lives in the present is the present moment of the past. A poet who acquires historical sense is conscious not of what is dead, but of what is "already living."

However, recent studies of Eliot suggest that he was "caught in the aporia of tradition versus innovation,"[36] or of the impersonal versus the personal, and his statements are inescapably cryptic if not inconsistent. In fact, Eliot himself was fully aware that he was confronting this aporia, as we can easily detect in his essay "The Use of Poetry." After stating that genuine taste is "inextricable from the development of personality and character,"[37] he adds in a footnote that he refuses to be drawn into any discussion of the definition of these two terms. Eliot asserts that poetry, though originating in the depths of the poet, is an expression not of personality, but of feelings and emotions that are extrapersonal. Yet he also attributes the superiority of Yeats's later works over his earlier ones to their greater expression of a unique personality, and explains his apparent contradiction in saying so by discussing the impersonality of craftsmanship and of the poet who turns his personal experience into an expression of general truths. Furthermore, when Eliot addresses Milton's influence on the English language, he declares that it is implicitly the personality of Milton that is in question, "not specifically his beliefs, or his language or versification, but the beliefs as realized in that particular personality, and his poetry as an expression of it."[38]

Obviously, Eliot knew that he was confronting an area in which all opposites simultaneously coexist, and Bloom, drawing upon Romanticism and the writings of Bate, knew it was the crossroads where he could meet Eliot as his Laius, Oedipus's father, and advise us to "clear our minds of Eliotic cant" and "give up the failed enterprise of seeking to understand any single poem as an entity in itself." Bloom realized that this aporia of tradition versus innovation, of text versus author, was the crossroads where he could establish his own difference and still be mistaken for his father. Bloom's idea that poetic influence deals with "the aboriginal poetic self"[39] can be seen as one side of a coin whose other side is Eliot's "sense of tradition." But, in his attempt to empty his precursor's reading of tradition, Bloom fails to realize that his own reading is not absolute, because it exists only as a difference. Eliot, Bate, and Bloom are all involved in Derrida's "scene of writing," which allows all to exist only as differences in a network of differential relationships. From these differences we can learn how to reconstruct our understanding of this aporia of tradition versus innovation or, in our case, of the Shakespearean originals versus Bond and Soppard's new versions.

Bloom applies his theory only to lyric form, but Bate recognizes the necessity of a theory of influence that can encompass all literary genres. Indeed, Bate, unlike Bloom, realizes that "the major Romantics never lost their healthful confidence that in or through the drama ... the open door could eventually be found.[40] The Romantics opened up the subjective world but "refused to view it as an end in itself."[41] Their greatest lyric poetry can be "described as an attempt to begin a new approach to drama."[42] Bate believes that the dramatic form is the rescue from that destruction of the aesthetic predicted by Bloom, because the dramatic form aspires to "a unity of being in which all the usual distinctions—objective, man and nature, intellect and feeling, conscious and unconscious—were ... only aspects or modes of the whole."[43] Bate informs us of Keats's habit of rereading Shakespeare's *King Lear* before beginning any new, large effort. Bate goes even further to speculate that

> Keats, if he had lived even to the age of fifty (and therefore had five times his active career of five years still before him at his disposal), would have fulfilled the hope he mentions (1819) after writing the odes, *Lamia*, and the *Fall of Hyperion*: that a few long poems, "written in the course of the next six years ... would nerve me up to the writing of a few fine Plays—my greatest ambition when I do feel ambitious.[44]

Despite Bate's success in showing how the Romantics faced up to the notion of originality, he seems to be intimidated by the fearful legacy of Shakespeare. Bate realizes that Shakespeare and his contemporaries were free to be and to do what they were and did because they were not yet shackled by our modern "petulant demand for originality."[45] They could look upon the mass of old plays as "waste stock, in which any experiment could be tried."[46] But Bate himself wonders,

> But what were you to do? Treat Shakespeare himself and other writers in the same spirit as only so much "waste stock"? You might in a moment of madness or desperation try to do so, or pretend to do so. But you could be sure that the sympathy of those around you would begin to chill, and you could understand why.[47]

It seems that when Bate made these remarks he was not aware that Tom Stoppard and Edward Bond, like many others before them, were engaged in the "mad and desperate" task of treating Shakespeare as "waste stock." In 1965, Stoppard started to write *Rosencrantz and Guildenstern Are Dead*. In August, 1967, the play was presented by the National Theatre at the Old Vic. In 1968, Bond began to conceive of his *Lear*. The play was first performed in September, 1971, by The Royal Court Theatre. These two plays consciously work with and against many of the concerns of Shakespeare. Dramatic criticism now needs to acknowledge, modify, and reconstruct the differences within the theory of influence so as to provide criteria by which we can decide how much of the two modern versions are original.

III

Given a frame simplified and reduced to its basic premise, Bloom's concept of influence can be useful for the purposes of this research. Bloom's notion of the scene of instruction can serve as the frame required. Bloom explains how writers pass from origins to repetitions and continuity and thence to the discontinuity that marks all revisionism. Since "every Primal Scene is necessarily a stage performance, or a fantastic fiction," Bloom considers his scene of instruction as primal for writers, just like Freud's two primal scenes of the Oedipal fantasy and of the slaying of a father by his rival sons. Bloom says that "behind any Scene of Writing, at the start of every textual encounter," there is an unequal love "where necessarily the giving famishes the receiver. The receiver is set on fire, and yet the fire belongs only to the giver."[48] In this scene of instruction, the writer has the compulsion to repeat the precursor's patterns in an attempt to "recover the prestige of origins,"[49] but "poetic repetition quests, despite itself, for the mediated vision of the fathers, since such mediation holds open the perpetual possibility of one's own sublimity, one's election to the realm of True Instructors."[50] This scene of instruction is founded upon an encounter trapped in time. The receiver tries to gain control over the text and be its first interpreter. Note the scene's "absolute firstness; it *defines* priority."[51]

Bloom's own view is that influence inescapably involves drastic distortion of the work of a predecessor:

> Poetic Influence—when it involves two strong, authentic poets—always proceeds by a misreading of the prior poet, an act of creative correction that is actually and necessarily a misinterpretation. The history of fruitful poetic influence, which is to say the main tradition of Western poetry since the Renaissance, is a history of anxiety and self-caricature, of distortion, of perverse, of willful revisionism.[52]

In Bloom's theory of influence, the dramatist is motivated to write when his imagination is seized upon by a work of a predecessor. The dramatist's attitude to his precursor, as in Freud's analysis of the Oedipal relation of son to father, is compounded not only of love and admiration, but also, since a strong dramatist has a compelling need to be autonomous and absolutely original, of hate, envy, and fear of the precursor's preemption of the son's imaginative space.

To safeguard his own sense of autonomy and priority, the dramatist swerves away from his precursor by executing a "corrective" movement in his own play, implying that the precursor's play proceeded accurately up to a certain point, but then should have swerved in the direction that the new play does. In the new play, the dramatist tries to antithetically complete his precursor's intention by retaining the parent-play's terms but meaning them in another sense, as though the precursor had failed to go far enough. In short, in his truly new play, the dramatist manages to move toward discontinuity with his precursor through an antithetical process.

In the following four chapters, I posit that Edward Bond, Tom Stoppard, and Shakespeare are engaged in Bloom's scene of instruction. We will try to answer these questions: How do the contemporary playwrights try in their own plays to move toward discontinuity with Shakespeare? In what ways do Bond and Stoppard work antithetically? In the words of Eliot, which are the "most individual parts" of Bond and Stoppard's works in which Shakespeare, their predecessor, asserts his immortality "most vigorously"? Where do those individual parts occur in Bond's *Lear* and Stoppard's *Rosencrantz and Guildenstern Are*

Dead? Hopefully, the answers to the above questions will help us not only to define the relationships between the two modern versions and the Shakespearean originals, but also to show much of the two new plays is original.

CHAPTER TWO

Bond versus Shakespeare

The basic difference between Shakespeare's *King Lear* and Bond's *Lear* is Bond's concern not only with the personal tragedies of the characters (Lear, Cordelia, Kent, Gloucester, and Edgar), but also with the tragedy of a society that revels in moralized and institutionalized patterns of aggression. Bond argues that Shakespeare, in spite of his original design, produced "a total arraignment of conventional authority and the morality used to explain and excuse it."[1] Justice as the antithesis of law and order is a central strand of Bond's *Lear*. "The play demonstrates one's rights, which can only be obtained in a society of justice and not one of law and order ... justice is the experience of liberation."[2]

Bond is a skillful and self-aware artist, well aware of his own aims, ideas, and methods. To some critics, he "has formulated a social philosophy more systematically than any dramatist since Shaw."[3] Bond's preparation for *Lear* was more extensive than it was for the plays he wrote before. His first public thoughts and notes about the play show not only an overpowering desire to escape from the shadow of Shakespeare, but also the development of an antithetical statement.

When Bond first conceived of writing his own version of *King Lear*, he approached Shakespeare's original with a skeptical and questioning spirit.

> I very much object to the worshipping of that play by the academic theatre ... because it is a totally dishonest experience. "Oh, yes, you know, this marvelous man suffering, and all the rest of it." I think that at the time it would have been a completely different experience to see Lear reacting in the Tudor set up ... Now, I think it's an invitation to be artistically lazy, to say, "Oh, how ... sensitive we are and this marvelous artistic experience we're having, understanding this play," and all the rest of it ... He's a Renaissance figure and he doesn't impinge on our society as much as he should ... I would like to rewrite the play to try to make it more relevant.[4]

Initially, Bond thought of excluding the figure of Lear himself. "If you get rid of the King, the play becomes much more interesting. He is a Renaissance preacher addressing himself to the Gods. He tells all the lies. He belongs to the seventeenth century, but he is irrelevant."[5] Yet, three months after beginning *Lear*, in October, 1979, Bond changed his mind and brought Lear back into his play.

> I'm not criticizing *King Lear* in any way. It's a play for which (It's a stupid thing to say) ... I have enormous admiration, and I've learnt more from it than from any

other play. But ... as a society we use the play in a wrong way. And it's for that reason I would like to rewrite it so that we now have to use the play for ourselves, for our society, for our time, for our problems.[6]

Bond's attention, as his notes on *Lear* indicate, was focused on the character Lear because he knew that Shakespeare's thesis about authority, law, and order was wholly based on that character. Bond realized that he could only swerve away from his precursor and proceed antithetically toward a movement of discontinuity if he dealt differently with the center of Shakespeare's world.

I can only say that Lear was standing in my path and I had to get him out of the way. I couldn't get beyond him to do other things that I also wanted, so I had to come to terms with him.[7]

In fact, it was more a question of Bond's coming to terms dialectically with his precursor, Shakespeare. Bond returned Lear to his version only to represent Shakespeare's thesis, now dominated by Bond's antithesis. In Bond's *Lear*, not only Lear and his evil daughters, but also Cordelia, are corrupted by the necessity of power. They are all caught in moralized and institutionalized patterns of aggression. Bond's urge to reinforce his thesis about violence and the need for justice compelled him to drastically change the character relationships in Shakespeare's play.

Cordelia in Shakespeare's *King Lear* aroused a strong hostile reaction in Bond: "one of the very important things in the play was to re-define the relationship between Cordelia and Lear. I don't want to make this seem easy or slick, but Cordelia in Shakespeare's play is an absolute menace. I mean she's a very dangerous type of person."[8] In his early notes for the play (January 21, 1970), Bond describes Cordelia as "a sort of unsuccessful Robespierre," the greatest destructive force on Lear. In Bond's play, Cordelia is not one of Lear's daughters. Bond changes their relationship, but significantly, keeps the name "Cordelia" for the counter-force that destroys Lear. Yet both Lear and Cordelia in Bond's play are defeated by their own concept of violence. Both perpetuate and moralize violence and the suppression of truth. What is important for Bond is not the question of inheritance and authority, but how society creates and perpetuates violence.

> It's not a question of inheritance, who gets to the top: it's to do with the total structure, the complete dance, the force that holds it together. In my play there can be no Albany waiting in the wings.[9]

The revolution of Bond's Cordelia demonstrates how one can use violence to reinforce the very things one initially revolted against. "Violence," Bond says, "has its own logistics and terror and fear will follow from its use. If the use is large (as in Stalin's regime) the terror and fear will be large and this will enforce the use of more violence."[10] For Bond, Cordelia is a Stalin-figure.

In the preface to *Lear*, Bond tries to define "our innate aggression," or as he conceives it, "our original sin." Though aggression is an "ability" and not a "necessity," human beings in our contemporary society have been caught in this vicious circle of organized and moralized violence. To Bond, human violence is more dangerous than the violence of animals.

> The predator hunting its prey is violent but not aggressive in the human way. It wants to eat, not destroy, and its violence is dangerous to the prey but not to the predator.

Animals only become aggressive—that is destructive in the human sense—when their lives, territory or status in their group are threatened, or when they mate or are preparing to mate. Even then the aggression is controlled. Fighting is usually ritualized, and the weaker or badly-placed animal will be left alone when it runs away or formally submits. Men use much of their energy and skill to make more efficient weapons to destroy each other, but animals have often evolved in ways to ensure they *can't* destroy each other. [11]

Bond believes that our society justifies, moralizes, and perpetuates aggression when it bases its whole structure on these "natural feelings of opposition"[12] inherent in human nature. Thus, society becomes an organization "held together by the aggression it creates."[13] Law and order are the means by which society justifies and maintains aggression, which eventually creates disruptive injustice. Power-politics, whether of the left or the right, are nothing but an institutionalized and legitimized form of injustice.

It is so easy to subordinate justice to power ... when this happens power takes on the dynamics and dialectics of aggression, and then nothing is really changed. Marx did not know about this problem, and Lenin discovered it when it was too late.[14]

To more directly bring home to us his radical concept of our "diseased culture," which he believes to be more relevant now than Shakespeare's concept of law and order, Bond goes further than Shakespeare does. To swerve away from his precursor he must confront him and use his material differently. In Shakespeare's

19

play, the mad Lear cries out in the hovel, "Then let them anatomise Regan, see what breeds about her heart. Is there any cause in nature that makes these hard hearts?" Accepting the challenge, in *Lear*, Bond answers this despairing question by taking Shakespeare's idea and creating a concrete scene of violence. Bond "anatomises" Fontanelle to show that human existence is nothing but an act of violence.

Lear: So much blood and bits and pieces packed in with all that care. Where is the ... where ? ... Where is the beast? The blood is as still as a lake ... Where? Where?

4ᵗʰ Prisoner: What's the man asking?

Lear: She sleeps inside like a lion and a lamb and a child. The things are so beautiful. I am astonished. I have never seen anything so beautiful. If I had known she was so beautiful ... how I would have loved her ... Did I make this—and destroy it? ... I knew nothing, saw nothing, learned nothing! Fool! Fool! Worse than I knew.

He puts his hands into Fontanelle and brings them out with organs and viscera. The soldiers react awkwardly and ineffectually.

Look at my dead daughter! ... I killed her! Her blood is on my hands! Destroyer! Murderer! And I must begin again. I must walk through my life, step after step, I must walk in weariness and bitterness, I must become a child, hungry and stripped and shivering in blood. I must open my eyes and see![15]

In contrast to Brecht, I think it's necessary to disturb an audience emotionally, to involve them emotionally in my plays, so I've had to find ways of making that "agro-effect" more complete. … which is in a sense to surprise them.[16]

Bond used and developed his "agro-effect" technique in all his plays before *Lear*. In each of his plays—*The Pope's Wedding, Saved, Early Morning*, and *Narrow Road to The Deep North*—he develops his concept of moralized violence and juxtaposes a cluster of powerful theatrical images which, indeed, genuinely reinforce his uncompromising radical vision. In *Lear*, he seems to have perfected both his ends and means.

Bond's agro-effect has been severely attacked by many critics. Indeed, because of this technique Bond has been "subjected to perhaps the most violent storm of protest and denigration aimed at any dramatist since Ibsen."[17] In fact, the hostility that greeted *Saved* paralleled the first English response to Ibsen's *Ghosts*.

We can properly understand Bond's technique and use of violence in the theatre when we compare it to Peter Brook's view of the use of violence in the theatre as discussed in his book *The Empty Space*.

Take the shocking atrocity stories, or the photo of the napalmed child, these shocks are the roughest of experiences—but they open the spectators' eyes to the

21

need for an action which in the event they somehow sap. It is as though the fact of experiencing a need vividly quickens the need and quenches it in the same breath. What then can be done?

I know of one acid test in the theatre. And it is literally an acid test. When a performance is over, what remains? Fun can be forgotten, but powerful emotion also disappears and good arguments lose their thread. When emotion and argument are harnessed to a wish from the audience to see more clearly into itself—then something in the mind burns. The event scorches on to the memory an outline, a taste, a smell—a picture. It's the play's central image that remains, its silhouette, and if the elements are highly blended, this silhouette will be its meaning, this shape will be the essence of what it has to say. When years later I think of a strikingly theatrical experience I find a kernel engraved in my memory: two tramps under a tree, an old woman dragging a cart, a sergeant dancing ... I haven't a hope of remembering the meanings precisely, but from the kernel I can reconstruct a set of meanings. Then a purpose will have been served. A few hours could amend my thinking for life. This is almost but not quite impossible to achieve.[18]

Brook's words shed light on an essential part of Bond's originality. In his notes on *Lear*, Bond's search for what "burns in the mind" is evident: "My own version of *Lear* ... isn't enough. I must start from my own image, and not merely my own ideas ... the reversal of the academic moral/artistic/theatrical myth isn't enough, the making *reality* of Lear mythology isn't enough, because the play isn't to get its life merely from being a commentary on *King Lear*, or an attack on it or correction of it. The play must have a structure rooted in itself, which then throws light across onto *King Lear*. The play must be its own dynamo and experience.[19]

Bond's attempt to free himself from Shakespeare, to bring about a movement of discontinuity and antithetically to dominate his precursor's text, is demonstrably apparent in *Lear*. In the following chapter we will examine the dramatic structure of *Lear*, its imagery, and its characters to identify the differences through which Bond sought to be the dominant interpreter.

CHAPTER THREE

Discontinuity and the Dominance of Antithesis

In the preface to *Lear*, Bond offers a thematic summary of his play's dramatic structure: "Act One shows a world dominated by myth. Act Two shows the clash between myth and reality, between superstitious men and the autonomous world. Act Three shows a resolution of this, in the world we prove real by dying in it."[1]

Shakespeare uses the Gloucester subplot to underscore the main plot's significances and thus intensify the tragic effect. Bond, to establish and reinforce his antithetical statement, not only ignores the entire Gloucester subplot, but also embeds the thesis of *King Lear*'s main plot in Act 1 of *Lear*. Bond's antithetical statement is extraordinarily intensified by the one-sided structure and by the development of scenes of the whole drama. Horst Oppel and Sandra Christenson observe that "the tectonic structure" of Bond's drama "rests chiefly upon the fundaments of parallel and contrasting scenes. There is hardly a single scene in *Lear* which does not have a special function in the whole fabric of the dramatic structure; each one, in its own way, contributes to the illumination of the demoniac interplay between violence and counter-violence."[2] Using variation and creative repetition, Bond compels us to succumb to "the inescapable conclusion that there is no more room for humanity in a world which is founded only on the interplay between violence and counter-violence."[3] His technique, therefore, is not a stagnant repetition, but a continuous experiment in probing the depths of misfortunes that transform people into slaves."[4]

The myth of Act 1 concerns Lear's blinkered refusal to see and understand what is happening around him. From the very beginning, Bond presents him as a king exercising absolute authority at the moment of his own displacement. He creates the conditions of his own overthrow. If Shakespeare's Lear abandons his authority by dividing his kingdom, Bond's Lear is an authority figure overtaken by revolutionary violence.

Lear begins with the arrival of Lear to inspect the progress of laborers forced to build a wall to protect his kingdom. Lear's great enterprise, his lifetime's work, has been the building of this great wall to keep his enemies out and his allies in. He says, "I started this wall when I was young. I stopped my enemies in the field, but there were always more of them. How could we ever be free? So I built this wall to keep our enemies out. My people will live behind this wall when I'm dead. You may be governed by fools but you'll always live in peace. My wall will make you free."[5]

The workers and soldiers in the first scene live in fear of Lear because he "always comes looking for trouble." But he does not come intending to shoot the worker wrongly suspected of sabotage. Nor do his daughters, Bodice and Fontanelle, intend to tell their father of their impending marriages to his enemies, the Duke of North and the Duke of Cornwall. Bond is careful to make the outcome of the scene grow directly from events in it. Lear himself precipitates events and creates the conditions of his own overthrow by deliberately using the accidental death of a worker to force the pace of work on the wall, "otherwise my visit's wasted." Lear's actions are those of a man utterly convinced of his own rightness. To protect his people, to put into effect what he has learned from history and his life, he makes the shooting of one worker an insignificant irritation. The tragic irony of the scene is given an additional savage twist by Lear's shooting the worker and in the same breath proclaiming his love for his people.

Lear: My enemies will not destroy my work! I gave my life to these people. I've seen armies on their hands and knees in blood, insane women feeding dead children at their empty breasts, dying men spitting blood at me with their last breath, our brave young men in tears—But I could bear all this! When I'm dead my people will live in freedom and peace and remember my name, no—venerate it! … They are my sheep and if one of them is lost I'd take fire to hell to bring him out. I loved and cared for all my children …

He shoots THIRD WORKER, and his body slumps forward on the post in a low bow.

There's no more time, it's too late to learn
anything.[6]

The first scene of Bond's *Lear* shows Lear acting with complete
autocratic authority. Therefore, he is outraged when, for the first
time, he is publicly contradicted by his own daughters. He does
not realize that the moment he shoots the worker is seen by
his daughters as the moment of disassociation. He cannot relate
cause to effect and understand that by murdering the worker, he
is responsible for what his daughters are or will be. Instead, he
resorts to childish tears in his rage against them.

To understand what he has done, and to learn, ultimately at the
cost of his life, the true nature of his society and the folly of its
power structure, Bond's Lear has a long distance to travel. First,
he is to overthrown by a similar act of violence. Bond says, "I
begin at the revolution."[7] In the first four scenes of the play, the
consequences of Lear's actions play out in the revolt of Bodice and
Fontanelle, who overthrow him. Act I, scene ii shows the essential
changes of circumstance that depose him. Lear's reliance on the
old strategy that defeated the fathers of North and Cornwall
seems archaic. Still he is unable to relate cause to effect. He
wonders aloud about his daughters, "Where does their vileness
come from?"[8] In scenes 3 and 4, Bond introduces elements of
black farce, which some critics consider an essential characteristic
of the dramatic devices he uses to prepare the ground for his own
exploration of violence and oppression. In *Early Morning*, for
instance, the theme of cannibalism is first introduced farcically:
Len and Joyce stand trial for eating a man while queuing outside
the Kilburn Empire to see a film called *Policeman in Black Nylons*.
Then cannibalism gradually becomes the central image for men
devouring and destroying each other. It is a technique "that goes

as far back in British drama as the medieval miracle plays, wherein the Towneley play *Secunda Pastorum* the farcical sheep-stealing and mock nativity precede and strengthen the serious and real nativity."[9] In *Lear*, Fontanelle and Bodice are presented as "figures of black farce, figures out of Jarry's *Ubu Roi*, childishly indulging their cruelties and sexual appetites."[10] After initiating the revolution by contracting marriages with their father's enemies, the North and Cornwall, they complain in bitter asides of their husbands' sexual incompetence. Fontanelle says, "When he gets on top of me I'm so angry I have to count to ten. That's long enough. Then I wait till he's asleep and work myself off. I'm not making do with that for long." Similarly, Bodice says, "Virility! It'd be easier to get blood out of a stone, and far more probable. I've bribed a major on his staff to shoot him in the battle."[11] This element of black farce becomes more apparent in scene 4 when Warrington is tortured. His tongue already cut out, he is methodically beaten while Bodice calmly knits and Fontanelle jumps up and down in perverse childlike merriment.

> *Fontanelle*: O, Christ, why did I cut his tongue out? I want to hear him scream … smash his hands … kill his feet … kill him inside! Make him dead! Father, Father! I want to sit on his lungs!
>
> *Bodice*: Plain, purl, plain. She was just the same at school.[12]

Bond deliberately uses these black farce and grotesque elements immediately before moving to confront directly, not in distorted caricature, the intolerable extremities of violence at the end of Act 1. Lear, overthrown by Fontanelle and Bodice, seeks refuge in the pastoral world of the gravedigger's boy and his wife. But the pastoral dream turns into a nightmare; Lear brings his madness and the threat of destruction to the simple world of the gravedigger's boy and his wife. In the last scene of Act 1, the soldiers capture the escaped king, kill the boy, and rape his wife. The pastoral alternative is shattered as the wife is raped and the boy is shot, and a blood stain spreads over the white sheet he is clasping around himself. It is here we realize for the first time that the wife's name is Cordelia. The withholding of Cordelia's name until the end of Act 1 marks the point at which Bond "emphatically thrusts Shakespeare's play well into the background of his own play."[13] Indeed, this is precisely where we recognize Bond's attempt to assert the movement of discontinuity with Shakespeare. The first four scenes of Act 1 contain insistent echoes of Shakespeare: the ingratitude of Lear's daughters and Lear's madness. To exorcise these Shakespearean echoes, Bond not only introduces the violence of the two daughters on a farcical level, but also moves to the pastoral setting where the serious and more horrible act of violence takes place. Furthermore, before we are told that the wife of the gravedigger's boy is called Cordelia, we discover that although she is not Lear's daughter in this play, she, like Lear, wants to "put a fence" around herself and her husband, and to "shut everyone else out."[14] Bond provides her with a different kind of life, but keeps her name to imply similarities between herself and Lear. Given her education and what she sees in the world around her, she, like Lear, applies her logic and becomes a source of counter-violence. Therefore, Cordelia and her world in Bond's *Lear* are a variation of the themes of violence pervading Bond's play. At the end of Act 1, when the pastoral dream turns into a nightmare, Bond's strong individual presence asserts itself and the very different direction of his play begins to emerge.

In Act 2, Bond opens up his contemporary world of dream and nightmare, of purgatorial suffering through which Lear must pass to achieve sanity and understanding. In a succession of powerful, haunting scenes, Bond dramatizes Lear's recognition that Bodice and Fontanelle are his daughters—they have been formed by his activity, they are children of his state, and he is totally responsible for them.[15] Put through a trial run by Bodice, Lear refuses to recognize either his daughter or his own reflection in a mirror handed to him.

> *Lear*: How ugly that voice is that's not my daughter's voice. It sounds like chains on a prison wall ... And she walks like something struggling in a sack.

> *Lear glances down briefly at the mirror.*

> No, that's not the king ... This is a little cage of bars with an animal in it ... No, no, that's not the king ... who shut that animal in that cage? Let it out. Have you seen its face behind the bars? There's a poor animal with blood on its head and tears running down its face.[16]

Lear becomes lost in his speculations and his daughters continue to goad him. Bodice says she will "polish" the mirror every day and see "it's not cracked." Fontanelle, seeing Lear's tears, relives her enjoyment of Warrington's torture. Lear's vision of injustice gradually broadens, so that in his last two lines of scene 1, he suggests that he hears "*all* the victims cry, all the people who ever passed through the courtroom."[17] But although he can see the blood of the victims of the daughters' injustice, he is not yet ready to recognize his own responsibility. He attributes cruelty to his daughters, or as he puts it, to the monsters who have replaced them: "My daughters have been murdered and these monsters have taken their place! I hear all their victims cry, where is justice?"[18] In scene 2, Lear goes to his cell still agitated about the trial, and says, "I must forget," because he knows he will go mad if he does not. Bond said that "the secret of playing the scene is to consider [act 2 scenes 1 and 2] as one scene for Lear"[19] as he tries in various ways to distance himself from the animal he has seen in the mirror. Preoccupied as he is with the imminent destruction of the world, he takes very little notice of the Ghost of the gravedigger's boy, who enters the cell. The Ghost is always there when Lear wants to escape from reality and responsibility. It is the Ghost who calls up the ghosts of Lear's daughters, who pathetically demonstrate why they are the way they are, and showing us how far back Lear's mistakes reach.

This scene is dramatically significant because it explains how much family and society are responsible for shaping or misshaping children. At this point, Lear can see an end to the pain in a vision of the future—but the vision slips away as soon as it is established when he is confronted by the Old Orderly, one of his own victims. The Old Orderly has been imprisoned for years, though he was a "survivor" who never challenged anyone directly. He is a victim of the pattern of violence that Lear initiated: "I come in 'ere thousands a years back, 'undreds a thousands. I don't know what I come in for. I forgot. I 'eard so many tell what they come in for it's all mixed up in me 'ead. I 'eard every crime in the book confessed t'me. Must be a record. Don't knew which was mine now. Murder? Robbin'? Violence? I'd like t'know. Just t'put me mind t' It's all gone. Long ago. The records is lost. 'Unrest. Satisfy me conscience. But no one knows now. 'undreds a years back." [20]

The Old Orderly is one of the people Lear saw dragged through the courtroom while on trial. But Lear cannot make the connection, and instead, retreats to the Ghost, another of his victims. For the first time in the scene, Lear really sees the Ghost, sees what he has destroyed. He must live with the dead of his creation before he can feel compassion for others.

Ghost: Let me stay with you, Lear. When I died I went somewhere. I don't know where it was. I waited and nothing happened. And then I started to rot, like a body in the ground. Look at my hands, they're like an old man's. They're withered. I'm young but my stomach's shriveled up and the hair's turned white. Look, my arms ! Feel how thin I am. (*Lear doesn't move.*) Are you afraid to touch me?

Lear: No.

Ghost: Feel.

Lear: (*hesitates, feels*). Yes, thin.

Ghost: I'm afraid. Let me stay with you, keep me here, please.

Lear: Yes, yes, poor boy. Lie down by me. Here. I'll hold you. We'll help each other. Cry while I sleep, and I'll cry and watch you while you

sleep. We'll take turns. The sound of the
human voice will comfort us.[21]

The scene ends with the Lear and the Ghost, the cause and the
effect, holding each other in a "frightening tableau." Yet this
is only the beginning of the nightmare. Act 2 leaves Lear and
the Ghost to show us the effect of the civil war upon Cordelia,
who has become the leader of a guerrilla army, and upon the
forces of Bodice and Fontanelle. Two brief scenes of revolution
and counter-revolution are set in the rival camps. At once, we
can see clearly where Cordelia's circumstances have brought her;
violence and power have turned her into a woman of absolute
determination. Like Lear at the beginning of the play, she calmly
asserts the necessity of shooting a wounded soldier because he has
become useless to the guerrillas. She finds his death regrettable
but inevitable in order to achieve power. In a letter dated March
18, 1977, Bond tersely stated,

Cordelia represents Stalin, it's as simple as that ... The
simple fact is that if you behave violently, you create an
atmosphere of violence, which generates more violence.
If you create a violent revolution, you always create a
reaction ... Lenin thinks for example that he can use
violence for specific ends. He does not understand that he
will produce Stalin, and indeed must produce a Stalin.[22]

The rapid and tense movement of Act 2 shows us the mechanics of
violence. In scene 4, Bodice and Fontanelle are shown as puppets
in a vicious circle of violence. Each has become both victim and
aggressor. For the conclusion of the act, Bond returns us to the
prison and the caged animals within it. Now, a chain of prisoners

moves along a country road; Lear is one of the chain gang. Then the defeated Fontanelle, is added to the chain, and in turn, manacled. She has been captured by Cordelia's forces, who have taken control. Lear is still in full retreat from the animal in the mirror; massively self-absorbed, he does not recognize Fontanelle at first. But the grimmer reality of political execution and the ever-present risk of violence leading to more violence force him outside his self-centered thoughts. Fontanelle is shot, and a prisoner who is a doctor, seeking to demonstrate his usefulness to the new regime, prepares an autopsy on Fontanelle's body. Lear is shocked when he sees his daughter's corpse.

> He expects to find something hideous but can't ... now he sees a human being for the first time. It's important to Lear that he finds something hideous. He's killed thousands of people fighting her because she was wicked. But he can't find anything hideous. He should be insistent that she was cruel and angry and hard ... When he says, 'If I had known she was so beautiful,' it is a rejection of everything he's ever said or ever done—he wouldn't have built the wall ... etc.[23]

Lear's shock grows as he takes his full place in the scene, and truths are pushed further home to him when Bodice is brought into the cell. He shows his remaining daughter the organs and viscera of her sister. Bodice tries pathetically to avoid her sister's fate, and ironically, demands justice in court. But things revert back to normal with her prolonged and messy death. At that moment, Lear finds his answer to the question posed in Shakespeare's play. There is no cause in nature for these hard hearts. It is man, not nature, that makes these hard hearts. Lear then takes upon himself a complete, almost Christ-like responsibility for man's destructiveness. He can now see what he has done.

> *Lear*: Look! I killed her! Her blood is on my hands! Destroyer! Murderer! And now I must begin again. I must walk through my life, step after step, I must walk in weariness and bitterness. I must become a child hungry and stripped and shivering in blood, I must open my eyes and see![24]

Aptly, however, Bond ends the act with a crowning act of violence: Lear is savagely and "scientifically" blinded by the prisoner-doctor. Though Bond has neglected Gloucester's story in Shakespeare's play, he retains the idea of blindness and insight to reinforce his own thesis. Lear's blindness is a theatrical conceit with which Bond forces together the concepts of power and cruel blindness, a self-imprisonment associated with authority. Like Gloucester, who "stumbled" when he "saw," Lear in Bond's play is blinded, and this cruelty affects his capacities radically as he begins to understand. He has to learn again how to act as a man and a politician. Only at this last stage of the act does the Ghost enter to help Lear out of the cell. Bond takes Lear back to the play's opening scene, near his wall, where he encounters his victims. Outraged by the news that Cordelia is rebuilding the wall and thus perpetuating violence, he kneels by the wall and admits the sum of his mistakes.

> *Lear*: I am the King! I kneel by this wall. How many lives have I ended here? … Men destroy themselves and say it's their duty? It's not possible! How can they be so abused? Cordelia

doesn't know what she's doing! I must tell her—write to her … I can't be silent.[25]

Bond's Cordelia becomes the Lear of Act 1. She insists as he once did that building the wall is an essential part of the power game; she has the same conviction that she is the savior of her people. But Lear is now another figure in the play. He has earned the right to know the truth. What he chooses to do with this knowledge is the theme of Act 3.

For Bond's Lear, "ripeness is not all." He resolves to commit himself to action. The first three scenes of Act 3 show Lear formulating his plan of action. He has developed skill at speaking the truth, but he now realizes that articulating the truth is useless. Instead of undergoing a reconciliation with Cordelia (as in Shakespeare's play), he decides to confront her as the new head of the people's government. Though Bond establishes her reasons and allows her a conscience in this confrontation, Cordelia admits her failure and Lear recognizes his strength. He exposes the mentality of violence.

Lear: Listen, Cordelia. You have two enemies, lies *and* the truth. You sacrifice truth to destroy lies, and you sacrifice life to destroy death. It isn't sane. You squeeze a stone till your hand bleeds and call that a miracle. I'm old, but I'm as weak and clumsy as a child, too heavy for my legs. But I've learned this, and you must learn it or you'll die. Listen, Cordelia. If a God had made the world, might would always be right, that would be so wise, we'd be spared so much suffering. But we made the world out of our smallness and weakness. Our lives are awkward and fragile and we have only one thing to keep us sane: pity, and the man without pity is mad.

Cordelia: You only understand self-pity. We must go back, the government's waiting ... We have other opponents, more ruthless than you. In this situation a good government acts strongly. I knew you wouldn't co-operate, but I wanted to come and tell you this before we put you on trial: we'll make the society you only dream of.

Lear: It's strange that you should have me killed, Cordelia, but it's obvious you would. How simple! Your Law always does more harm than crime, and your morality is a form of violence.[26]

Significantly, this confrontation takes place immediately before the last scene of Bond's play. While Shakespeare starts his drama with that confrontation, Bond chooses to present it just before taking us to the audacious climax of his play. Bond reverses the structure of *King Lear* to imply that Shakespeare's play does not have a confrontation dealing with the basis of Bond's antithetical statement. In Bond's play, fear forces Lear and Cordelia to build the wall and thus perpetuate the pattern of moralized violence. For Bond, fear, not filial ingratitude or inheritance, is deeply rooted in human nature. Indeed, the confrontation scene in Bond's play marks the completion of that movement of discontinuity with

Shakespeare. Now, Bond can move to the place he thinks his precursor failed to reach. In Bond's *Lear*, the confrontation with Cordelia is Lear's crucial turning point. In the early scenes of Act 3, we see him as a Tiresias-like figure preaching in parables to the people who come to hear him. But after the confrontation, Lear realizes that this phase of resignation, of ripe wisdom, is over. He has a journey to go on and an act to perform. The play's final scene shows Lear at the wall, as in the opening scene, but acting in a different way. Instead of sacrificing a life to build the wall, Lear now sacrifices his own life to unbuild it. Lear sets to work with his bare hands and a shovel to tear down the wall that was his life's work and that Cordelia is perpetuating now. He is shot by one of the junior officers. The ending of the play is splendidly dramatic; it gathers the play's meaning into a final symbolic action. It is the inevitable climatic movement toward which everything in the play has been leading.

A powerful dramatic device that helped Bond to create his movement of discontinuity and underscore the dominance of his antithetical statement is theatrical imagery. Leslie Smith believes that Bond's *Lear* is more successful than Eliot's dramas because Bond's "poetry of the theatre is not dependent on verse: it functions through the concrete action and the physical images of the drama."[27] Bond himself said, "What I begin from is a series of small visual images ... when I write, the rhythm—the whole concentration of the writing—requires action. Finally somebody has to get up and do something."[28] Bond's *Lear* begins and ends with the killing of a man working on the wall. It is one of the central images of oppression and confinement in the play. This image "brilliantly evokes both an ancient landscape and a modern one: we think at one and the same time of the Berlin wall and the Cold War; and of the massive earthworks near Bond's home called

Devil's Dyke and Fleam Dyke thrown up by the East Anglians after the departure of the Romans to protect themselves from marauders."[29] Bond begins his play with Lear's tour of inspection in which he could be seen as "any contemporary field marshal or bellicose politician claiming to defend the peace by preparing for war, and calling self-imprisonment freedom."[30] From the very beginning of the play, the wall imposes its dark shadow over the action.

Another image central to Bond's meaning is the that of a man as caged animal. This image reverberates beyond the immediate context and relates to the governed as much as the governors; the people and the rulers alike are imprisoned within a social and political structure that does not fill their real reads. It is notable that Bond uses and develops this image precisely where he tries to assert the movement of discontinuity with Shakespeare and the dominance of his own thesis. Act 1, for instance, ends with the caged animals, a chain of prisoners moving along a country road. The chain includes Lear, Fontanelle, and their victims. It is a vivid theatrical metaphor for the meaning of the play: a vicious circle of violence and oppression in which governors and the governed, tyrants and victims, end up chained to each other.

Physical theatrical imagery is Bond's main dramatic tool not only for relating the meaning of his play to its structure, but for escalating the intensity of the dramatic movement. In Act 1, the death of the gravedigger's boy and the rape of his wife are accompanied by the sound of pigs squealing as they are slaughtered offstage. This combination of visual and auditory effects recurs immediately before Lear is shot in the brief but powerful ending of the play. From offstage sounds "the distant squealing of angry pigs, further off than at the end of Act One … the ghost stumbles in. It is covered with blood. The pig squeals slowly die out."[31] Gored and trampled by the pigs, the Ghost drops dead at Lear's feet as the squealing finally stops. Now, the auditory imagery gives way to the imagery of light, of clear vision, and of an understanding that Lear requires before performing his last act: "I see my life, a black tree by a pool. The branches are covered with tears. The tears are shining with light. The wind blows the tears in the sky. And my tears fall down on me."[32]

Besides the main characters, Bond presents a group of minor characters who represent the common man and corrupted innocence. These minor figures are not much more than representatives of specific behavior patterns and power constellations in society. While Bond gives his main characters names, he reduces most of the other characters to the titles of their function in society, with no further differentiation than the numerical or alphabetical order of their appearance on stage. For Bond, these minor characters are mere functionaries of the system, thereby losing their individuality or personal identity. Workers on the wall, soldiers, prisoners, and farmers are all alike: they help perpetuate injustice, either through a passive acceptance of the given social morality and of their duty to it, or through an active participation in injustice with the hope of personal advantage. They are all guilty of aggression and violence. Significantly, Lear is shot by the farmer's son, whom Lear once tried to preserve from the clutches of the vicious circle of violence.

To sum up: in the new textual encounter *Lear*, Bond's attempt to be the dominant interpreter, or, to use Bloom's words, the fire-giver, is evident. The few details that we have examined in the dramatic structure, theatrical imagery, and characters of

Lear substantiate our conclusion that Bond's play has the two qualities that distinguish a really original work: the movement of discontinuity with the precursor and the dominance of the dramatist's antithetical statement.

CHAPTER FOUR

Stoppard and Influence

The theoretical perspective of this study exposes some inadequacies in the vocabulary some critics use to describe the composition of Stoppard's *Rosencrantz and Guildenstern Are Dead*. Ruby Cohn, for instance, says that Stoppard proved "extremely skillful in dovetailing the *Hamlet* scenes into the Godot situation." Charles Marowitz writes, "Stoppard displays a remarkable skill in juggling the données of existential philosophy." Thomas Whitaker suggests "the *raisonneur* of this clever pastiche is of course The Player—who knowingly plays himself."[1] Such language—"skillful dovetailing," "clever pastiche"—condemns while it praises. Not only does it fail to illuminate Stoppard's originality, it also subtly categorizes the play as a derivative piece of workmanship.

From the first time *Rosencrantz and Guildenstern Are Dead* was performed, critics have recognized its derivation from Shakespeare's *Hamlet* and Beckett's *Waiting for Godot*. They have noticed other influences as well; Pirandello, T. S. Eliot, Wilde, Kafka, and Pinter all left their literary or theatrical traces on the play, and Ludwig Wittgenstein's *Investigations* provided philosophical bearings. Stoppard himself is vague or noncommittal about some of these influences: "Prufrock and Beckett are the twin syringes of my diet, my arterial system ... I really wasn't aware of ... Pirandello as an influence. It would be very difficult to write a play which was totally unlike Beckett, Pirandello and Kafka."[2]

Stoppard's remarks might lead us to believe that allusions to writers other than Beckett and Shakespeare in *Rosencrantz and Guildenstern Are Dead* are unintentional or superficial. In fact, Stoppard admits his debt to *Waiting for Godot* is enormous: "there's just no telling what sort of effect it had on our society, who wrote because of it, or who wrote in a different way because of it ... Of course it would be absurd to deny my enormous debt to it, and love for it." Stoppard also emphasizes what he describes as "a Beckett joke,"[3] a technique Beckett uses in his plays: "It appears in various forms but it consists of confident statement followed by immediate refutation by the same voice. It's a constant process of elaborate structure and sudden—and total—dismantlement."[4]

Rosencrantz and Guildenstern Are Dead shows strong influence by *Waiting for Godot*. Both plays deal with two little men, lacking in power and knowledge, who grapple with a world full of uncertainty. Similarities in characterization and in the relationships between the two main characters in each play are easily recognizable. Guildenstern resembles Vladimir, who is prone to anguish because he has a livelier imagination than his partner, Estragon, who resembles Rosencrantz. Furthermore, the two plays share familiar theatrical and literary conventions: a minimal, localized scene; direct address to the audience; and dialogue full of puns, both serious and frivolous, which are integral to the meaning of the play.

Of course, there are basic differences between *Rosencrantz and Guildenstern Are Dead* and *Waiting for Godot*. They differ structurally in two respects. The structure of *Waiting for Godot* reflects the process of waiting; it is circular and repetitive. Critics have generally recognized that the play's two acts suggest a repeated rather than a completed action, and that the second act largely repeats the first. On the contrary, the structure of Stoppard's play is basically linear, with a completed action. The summons of Rosencrantz and Guildenstern at the beginning of the play leads to their involvement in the *Hamlet* plot, and finally, to their deaths. Another difference is that in *Waiting for Godot*, Vladimir and Estragon generate their own action of waiting (whether or not Godot is coming), whereas in Stoppard's play, Rosencrantz and Guildenstern are trapped in the *Hamlet* plot through what seems to them to be a supernatural agency. They are bewildered by fast-moving developments in the *Hamlet* plot; they cannot understand why these sudden and unforeseen changes have occurred. Beckett's two tramps represent the universal experience of waiting. Stoppard's two principals represent the experience of feeling caught by an incomprehensible force in an odd tragedy "where everyone who is marked for death dies." Rosencrantz and Guildenstern wonder what are they to do without adequate instructions in their blank context. Yet, their context is not actually blank; it is the script of *Hamlet*. Their destiny is Shakespeare's script, which leads them to death. They are not, as William Babula says, "escapees from Shakespeare's tragedy, but victims, as Hamlet is a victim, of the story line."[5]

In Shakespeare's *Hamlet*, Rosencrantz and Guildenstern are a couple of characters so unimportant and marginal that they can be and sometimes are cut from productions of the play without noticeable difficulty. But in Stoppard's version, they are the pivot of the play. In the story of these two minor characters in *Hamlet*, Stoppard saw a situation that truly mirrors the absurdity of the human condition. Indeed, the absurdity is already present in Shakespeare's text. Stoppard's achievement lies in foregrounding the absurdity in his own play. Significantly, in the first published edition of the play in 1967, the action, the action is circular, much like that of *Waiting for Godot*. At the end, Rosencrantz and Guildenstern may be dead, but someone shouts and bangs on a shutter, indistinctly calling two names. In rehearsals at the National Theatre, Stoppard cut this ending, and in subsequent editions, Shakespeare has the last word.[6] Stoppard returns at the end of the play to the final scene of *Hamlet* echoing his play's title. This not only reminds us that the fate of Rosencrantz and Guildenstern is predetermined, but also implies that Stoppard has accepted Shakespeare's limitations—*Hamlet* functions as a frame. When asked why he made this choice, Stoppard answered that he had no other choice for this kind of drama. "He considers Shakespeare's tragedy 'probably the most famous play in any language; it is part of a sort of common mythology'; and Rosencrantz and Guildenstern 'are so much more than merely bit players in another famous play … As far as their involvement in Shakespeare's text is concerned they are told very little about what is going on and much of what they are told isn't true. So I see them much more clearly as a couple of bewildered innocents rather than a couple of henchmen.'"[7]

From the beginning, Stoppard viewed *Hamlet* as a means for solving practical problems of composition. The inevitability of the *Hamlet* plot is used by Stoppard as a device for denying choice in human affairs, and thus, asserting the major theme of his play: the absurdity of the human condition. Like Bond, who initially considered excluding the character Lear but later returned him to represent a minor theme dominated by a major antithetical statement in *Lear*, Stoppard returns the final scene of *Hamlet* to his play to serve his own purposes. Though the foundation of *Rosencrantz and Guildenstern Are Dead* is Shakespeare's play, everything noble and weighty in *Hamlet* Stoppard reduces to absurdity. In Stoppard's play, Hamlet becomes a slick conniver who drifts in and out, adding to the general confusion. The most significant exchanges and soliloquies in Shakespeare's play are eliminated and diluted with comedy so drastically abridged that they are mere reminiscences of Shakespeare's passages. At the same time, the focus shifts to *Hamlet*'s minor characters and action that takes place offstage in the original.

Just as Bond ignores the entire Gloucester subplot and embeds the thesis of *King Lear* in the first act of his play, Stoppard deliberately bases the dramatic structure of his play on the *Hamlet* plot to reinforce his major theme. Ionesco, the representative spokesman for the principles of absurd drama, has pointed out that "the conventional plot in its predictability and resolution is a reassuring distortion of life, whose primary law is unpredictability. A meaningful action, on the other hand, is one that captures and reflects on the absurd."[8]

Despite the apparent derivativeness recognized in *Rosencrantz and Guildenstern Are Dead*, Stoppard is still recognizable as the dominant interpreter of the new textual encounter. His thesis is perhaps not drastically antithetical to Shakespeare's. Yet I would argue that Stoppard's vision is distinctly different from that of Shakespeare.

In *Hamlet*, Shakespeare exploits all possible dramatic means to position Hamlet at the core of the play. Thus, Hamlet, stands in the foreground of Shakespeare's text. Consequently, other characters and incidents revolve around him. Before Tom Stoppard wrote his version, most, if not all critics of *Hamlet* had been concerned with the character of Hamlet; if they even considered other elements of the play, they did so in relation to the protagonist. In his PhD dissertation, Paul S. Conklin investigates the growth of Hamlet criticism from 1601 through the year 1821, and concludes, "It need hardly be said that the character of the hero is the point of major consideration," and "sooner or later all roads lead to this focal point."[9] Claude C. H. Williamson compiled all readings on the character of Hamlet from 1661 until 1947 and from over one hundred sources to realize that "there is no single topic under the dramatic sun on which so many lances, quixotic and other, have been broken to no avail as *Hamlet*."[10] "To no avail," Williamson goes on, "because the windmills stand exactly where they stood in 1603, when Hamlet was born."[11]

Stoppard manages to break this pattern in his play through a brilliant inversion of Shakespeare's material. In the following chapter, I will explain how Stoppard establishes his own vision. We will examine the dramatic structure of characterization and theatrical imagery in *Rosencrantz and Guildenstern Are Dead* to identify the differences through which Stoppard sought to be the dominant interpreter of his new textual encounter.

CHAPTER FIVE

Foregrounding the Absurd

The story of Rosencrantz and Guildenstern occupies only a small portion of the dramatic structure of *Hamlet*. To make these two marginal characters the center of his play, Stoppard applies the same dramatic devices used by Shakespeare in *Hamlet*. Both dramatists manipulate the same tools for different ends. In the first scene of *Hamlet*, Shakespeare manages to create a mood of tension and suspense before we first see Hamlet. The scene holds the interest of the audience with its air of mystery and expectancy, the eeriness of the hour, and the quick entrance of the ghost. Hamlet is introduced by name when Bernardo, Francisco, Marcellus and Horatio decide to "impart" what they have seen "unto young Hamlet."[1] Shakespeare skillfully links the supernatural element with his protagonist. The second scene brings Hamlet closer to our attention and sympathy. Now the setting changes from tense apprehension under the night sky to the pomp and ceremony of the King's council chamber. In contrast to the nervous exchanges of the first scene is the courtly worldliness of life within the castle. The general corruption of the court serves to accentuate Hamlet's integrity. Claudius's speech is revealing; numerous figures of speech bringing together two opposing ideas—spoilt (defeat) and joy, mirth and death, dirge and marriage—make his long, formal speech sound impressive and befitting a king, but they also completely cover up his guilt.

> Therefore our sometime sister, now our queen,
> The imperial jointress of this warlike state,
> Have we, as 'twere with a defeated joy—
> With one auspicious, and one dropping eye,
> With mirth in funeral, and with dirge in marriage
> In equal scale weighing delight and dole
> Taken to wife.2

To marry his sister-in-law so soon after his brother's death is a dubious action; by using these fine phrases he tries to make it sound more forthright than it really is. The rest of the scene informs us that his councilors supported him when he married Hamlet's mother. Indeed, from the very beginning of Shakespeare's play, we are made to respond negatively to Claudius, Gertrude, and Polonius. Hamlet is thus placed at the center of our sympathy and interest, and he remains the focal point of the dramatic structure over the next eighteen scenes. When introducing Rosencrantz and Guildenstern for the first time (act 2 scene 2), Shakespeare significantly associates them with Claudius, to whom we have been responding negatively. Their first scene clearly indicates that Shakespeare has given them "a group characterization."3 Claudius's words, "use," "supply," and "profit," tell us that Rosencrantz and Guildenstern exist merely as tools in the hands of the court. Their first words also demonstrate this.

Rosencrantz: Both your majesties
>Might, by the sovereign power you have of us
>Put your dread pleasures more into command
>Than to entreaty.

Guildenstern: But we both obey
>And here give up ourselves in the full bent
>To be commanded.4

Claudius: Thanks, Rosencrantz and gentle Guildenstern

Gertrude: Thanks, Guildenstern and gentle Rosencrantz.5

Rosencrantz's answer is hardy different from Guildenstern's, and Claudius and Gertrude's words unmistakably establish their characters: they are submissive and indistinguishable. The fact that they have no identities and exist only as tools in the hands of Claudius and Gertrude, with whom we do not sympathize, makes us less sympathetic toward them. This explains why we tend to accept Hamlet's cruel words announcing their death (act 5, scene 2) without concern.

In Stoppard's play, the process is reversed. Hamlet is excluded from the plot exposition, and the ghost, that making-strange element used by Shakespeare to direct our attention to Hamlet, is entirely dispensed with. The first characters we see at the opening of Stoppard's play are Rosencrantz and Guildenstern. These characters, given a "group characterization" in *Hamlet*, are in this play given physical descriptions with minute detail. They are "well-dressed, hats, cloaks, sticks and all." While each of them has "a large leather money bag," Guildenstern's bag is "nearly empty" and Rosencrantz's "nearly full."6 However, these physical details alone do not impart any sense of individuality. We are told in the stage directions that "two Elizabethans" are "passing the time in a place without any visible character." Rosencrantz and Guildenstern are "betting the toss of a coin," and "they have apparently been doing this for some time." "Rosencrantz, whose bag is nearly full, "betrays no surprise at all—he feels none. However, he is nice enough to feel a little embarrassed at taking so much money off his friend. Let that be his character note." Guildenstern, who is losing all the time, "is not worried about the money." He is "aware but not going to panic about it—his character note."7 Under careful examination, these two characters are the same indistinguishable, submissive human beings we have seen in *Hamlet*. Dramatically, but farcically, Stoppard deliberately foregrounds the basic characteristics given to them by Shakespeare.

> *Ros*: My name is Guildenstern, and this is Rosencrantz.
> (*Guil confers briefly with him.*)
> (*without embarrassment.*) I'm sorry— his name's Guildenstern, and I'm Rosencrantz.
>
> *Claudius*: Welcome, dear Rosencrantz ...(*he raises a hand at Guil. while Ros bows—Guil bows late and hurriedly.*) ... and Guildenstern.
> (*He raises a hand at Ros while Guil bows to him—Ros is still straightening up from his previous bow and half way up he looks down*

again. With his head down, he twists to look at Guil, who is on the way up.)

Claudius: Thanks, Rosencrantz (*turning to Ros who is caught unprepared, while Guil bows*) and gentle Guildenstern (*turning to Guil who is bent double*).

Gertrude (*correcting*): Thanks, Guildenstern (*turning to Ros, who bows as Guil checks upward movement to bow too—both bent double, squinting at each other*) ... and gentle Rosencrantz. (*Turning to Guil, both straightening up—Guil checks again and bows again.*)8

Besides providing comic effect, these dramatic beats show us that Rosencrantz and Guildenstern are still the same characters we have seen in *Hamlet*. Unlike Bond, who changes the relationship between Lear and Cordelia, Stoppard keeps the relationships as they are in Shakespeare's text to reinforce his major theme. Stoppard does not try to bring about a movement of discontinuity with his precursor, but brings to the foreground of his version Rosencrantz and Guildenstern's characteristics. Stoppard uses Shakespeare's limitations in his own play to show how and why the human condition is essentially and inescapably absurd. Though the story of Rosencrantz and Guildenstern is a fringe event in *Hamlet*, it is in itself a highly ironic and fundamentally dramatic situation, which Stoppard rewrites in three acts to a different end.

One aspect of Stoppard's novelty lies in his successful development of the play within a play. Significantly, Stoppard introduces the troupe of players before Rosencrantz and Guildenstern meet any of the other characters from *Hamlet*. In *Hamlet*, these players disappear immediately after Claudius says, "Give me some light! Away!" (act 3, scene 2). But in *Rosencrantz and Guildenstern Are Dead*, the players, specialists in illusion, are present in all three acts and meaningfully connect with Rosencrantz and Guildenstern. In Act 1, Stoppard establishes swiftly but subtly the similarity between his protagonists' situation and the condition of the players. Before they meet the players, Rosencrantz and Guildenstern inform us that they have been spinning coins for as long as they can remember. Vaguely uneasy and uncertain as to which of them is Rosencrantz and which Guildenstern, they know only that they have been summoned to court. When they try to remember this event, they can recall only that "there was a messenger" and "they were sent for." Although there are many details that they do remember, they cannot precisely define that message. Rosencrantz remembers a "pale sky before dawn," and that "a man standing on his saddle to bang on the shutters" called their names. "It was urgent—a matter of extreme urgency, a royal summons." He recalls "lights in the stable yard," and being fearful lest they "come too late." When Guildenstern asks him, "Too late for what?" he answers, "How do I know?" These two are like "a man breaking his journey between one place and another at a third place of no name, character, population or significance." And this is also, precisely, the condition of the players. They are all "traveling" people.

Guil:	Where from?
Player:	Home. We're traveling people. We take our chances where we find them.
Guil.	It was chance, then?
Player:	Chance?
Guil.:	You found us.
Player:	Oh yes.
Guil.:	You were looking?
Player:	Oh no.
Guil.:	Chance, then.
Player:	Or fate.
Guil.:	Yours or ours?
Player:	It could hardly be one without the other. 9

Although the idea of employing different fictional levels might originate from the play within a play in *Hamlet*, Stoppard goes further by connecting Rosencrantz and Guildenstern and the players in a single world. Stoppard allows his two protagonists and the players to dominate the whole structure of the play.

By developing the relationship between Rosencrantz, Guildenstern, and the players, Stoppard not only obliterates all demarcation lines between different plays and worlds, but also unsettles his audience, compelling them to identify with his tragi-comic protagonists. This complex irony derives from the fact that Rosencrantz and Guildenstern, who boast of their superiority over the actors, are in actuality twice-removed from the reality of the audience (actors impersonate characters in Stoppard's play who are, in turn, based upon two characters from *Hamlet*). And yet, they are gradually shown to be human beings trapped in the circumstances in which they find themselves. The disreputable actors, on the other hand, "know which way the wind is blowing"[2] and can offer advice to the respectable courtiers, who are at a loss:

> *Guil*:   But for God's sake what are we supposed to *do*?

> *Player*:   Relax. Respond. That's what people do. You can't go through life questioning your situation at every turn.

> *Guil*:   But we don't know what's going on, or what to do with ourselves. We don't know how to *act*.

> *Player*:   Act natural ... Everything has to be taken on trust ... One acts on assumptions.11

Throughout Stoppard's play, Rosencrantz and Guildenstern are unaware that, like the players, they are employed at the court of Elsinore—however, the audience clearly sees them constantly revealing their natures. When they meet the troupe of players for the first time, they insist on a distinct division between actors and spectators. Guildenstern says, "I thought we were gentlemen."12 Both are convinced of their own superiority over the low "rabble," and are shocked at the suggestion of taking part in a performance of *The Rape of the Sabine Women*. They adopt a patronizing attitude toward the players.

> *Guil.:*   Perhaps I can use my influence.
>
> *Player:*   At the tavern?
>
> *Guil:*   At the court. I would say I have some influence.[3]

Although the Player treats Rosencrantz and Guildenstern as his prospective patrons, his remarks make us aware that they are not only spectators. In Act 2, they desperately try to avoid getting entangled in the action so as to maintain their position as spectators, never realizing that actor and spectator are interchangeable roles, "two sides of the same coin," or "the side of two coins." Not only their words but also their mimetic scenes underscore this dramatic irony by showing the protagonists as actors. Just before the players rehearse *The Murder of Gonzago*, Rosencrantz and Guildenstern practice for their encounter with Hamlet, with Guildenstern assuming the part of Hamlet, and perform the scene of their arrival in England, with Rosencrantz playing the English king. Thus, they unconsciously assume the role of actor, which they earlier resisted.

The scene in which Guildenstern and Rosencrantz watch the rehearsal of *The Mousetrap* is the most significant one in the play. The Player says, "Now if you wouldn't mind just moving back,"[4] implying that the spectators and actors have changed roles. While the disreputable players have established their superiority, Rosencrantz and Guildenstern become more and more insecure.

> *Player*:   I can come and go as I please.
>
> *Guil*:   You're evidently a man who knows his way around.
>
> *Player*:   I've been here before.
>
> *Guil*:   We're still finding our feet.
>
> *Player*:   I should concentrate on not losing your heads.[5]

When Rosencrantz and Guildenstern come face to face with their mirror-images, the two spies, they are still unwilling to recognize their own real selves.

> *Ros*:   Well, if it isn't—! No, wait a minute, don't tell me—it's a long time since—when was it? Ah, this is taking me back to—when was it? I know you, don't I? I never forget a face—(*he looks into the spy's face*) not that I know you, that is. For a moment I thought—no, I don't know you, do I? Yes, I'm afraid you're quite wrong. You must have mistaken me for someone else.

(Guil, meanwhile, has approached the other spy, brow creased in thought.)

Player: (*to Guil*) Are you familiar with this play?

Guil: No. [6]

Rosencrantz and Guildenstern insist on being spectators. Ironically, even their clapping at the performance foreshadows their tragic fate. What blinds them to reality and makes them stumble helplessly toward their fate is their illusion of their own status, the discrepancy between what they think they are and what they really are, which is pawns in the hands of the court. Indeed, here, precisely is a basic difference between Stoppard and Shakespeare. In *Hamlet*, just before the play within the play starts, this exchange occurs between Hamlet and Polonius:

Hamlet: (*to Polonius*) My lord, you played once i' the university, you say?

Polonius: That did I, my lord; and was accounted a good actor.

Hamlet: And what did you enact?

Polonius: I did enact Julius Caesar. I was killed i' the Capitol; Brutus killed me.

Hamlet: It was a brute part of him to kill so capital a calf there—Be the players ready?[7]

Like Rosencrantz and Guildenstern in Stoppard's play, Hamlet and Polonius in Shakespeare's play seem to miss the significance of their own words, which clearly foreshadow the death of Polonius. There is no real similarity between Polonius and Caesar, but Stoppard uses many dramatic devices to demonstrate how Rosencrantz and Guildenstern and the two spies—reality and illusion, real life and acted life, rehearsal and performance, spectator and actor—are two sides of the same coin. If Shakespeare guides us to distinguish reality from illusion in Hamlet, Stoppard, thoroughly developing the play-within-a-play theme, compels us to realize that the demarcation between reality and illusion is itself unreal. In contrast to Rosencrantz and Guildenstern, the players accept this paradox as fact.

> *Guil*:   Well … aren't you going to change into your costume?
>
> *Player*:   I never change out of it, sir.
>
> *Guil*:   Always in character.
>
> *Player*:   That's it.[8]

The recognition of this paradox must be deeply disturbing to a perceptive audience. The mood of detachment in which we have been watching the childish games of Stoppard's protagonists in Act 1 gradually gives way to a feeling of unease in Act 2. Stoppard's sophisticated use of mirror technique (the play within a play and other mimetic scenes) instills our anxiety not only about the freedom of Rosencrantz and Guildenstern, but also about our own understanding of the relationship between illusion and reality. By the end of Act 2, we have received many hints that the remoteness of the actuality of death is going to change. Rosencrantz and Guildenstern discuss their ability to conceive of their own deaths; they can imagine themselves alive in a box or coffin. The third act opens in silence and pitch darkness, suggesting the nothingness of death, which is a recurring theme in the final act of Stoppard's play. In this act, Stoppard introduces the theme of sea travel to reinforce the play-life metaphor. Rosencrantz assumes the role of the English king while Guildenstern plays both himself and Rosencrantz. We move from one level of unreality to another when they forget themselves and break the seal on Claudius's letter to find that it asks for Hamlet to be killed. At last, something depends on their choice. This supposed control over their three destinies, however, is only illusory: Hamlet overhears their conversation and substitutes the letter with one requesting their deaths. By then, Rosencrantz and Guildenstern have realized that they would not have been strong enough to interfere with Claudius's plot.

> *Guil:* Let us keep things in proportion … As Socrates so philosophically put it, since we don't know what death is, it is illogical to fear it. It might be … very nice. Certainly it is a release from the burden of life, and, for the godly, a haven and a reward. Or to look at it another way— we are little men, we don't know the ins and outs of this matter, there are wheels within wheels, etcetera—it would be presumptuous of us to interfere with the designs of fate or even of kings. All in all, I think we'd be well advised to leave well alone.[9]

Before the end of the play they discover Hamlet's forged letter. The players who are in the same boat as them form a menacing circle around the protagonists, and Guildenstern, snatching a dagger from the Player's belt, talks angrily about the difference between the reality of death and the theatrical illusion of it.

> Player: In our experience, most things end in death.
>
> Guil: (*fear, vengeance, scorn*): Your experience?— *Actors*! … I'm talking about death—and you've never experienced *that*. And you cannot *act* it. You die a thousand casual deaths … even as you die you know that you will come back in a different hat. But no one gets up after *death*—there is no applause—there is only silence and some second-hand clothes, and that's—*death*—
>
> (*And he pushes the blade in up to hilt. The Player stands with huge, terrible eyes, clutches at the wound as the blade withdraws: he makes small weeping sounds and falls to his knees.*)[10]

Yet this, too, turns out to be a theatrical death. The Player has already told us that when one of his actors was condemned to death and he arranged for the sentence to be carried out during a performance, the results were unconvincing. Even the death of Rosencrantz and Guildenstern is represented theatrically through a conjuring trick: they disappear into the upstage darkness just before the dialogue switches back to the sequence from *Hamlet*. Guildenstern's last words, "We'll know better next time," show that Stoppard is careful to be ambiguous about the reality of their death.

To differentiate between the world of his foregrounded characters (Rosencrantz and Guildenstern and the players) and the world of all the other characters, Stoppard employs a two-sided strategy. While all the other characters speak the same language that Shakespeare originally gave them, the foregrounded characters speak in modern English. If the poetic English of Elizabethan times makes Shakespeare's central characters seem to be moving purposefully toward a specific end, the language of the foregrounded characters shows them to be circumambulating. Language is one of Stoppard's methods of bringing home the absurdity of his central characters' world. The simplest statement or question can become a source of amazing perplexity.

Player: Why?

Guil: Ah. (*to Ros*) Why?

Ros: Exactly.

Guil: Exactly what?

Ros: Exactly why.

Guil: Exactly why what?

Ros: What?

Guil: Why?

Ros: Why what, exactly?[11]

Coin tossing and the long run of "heads" reveals an absurdist universe and foreshadows the unbreakable chain of events that will catch Rosencrantz and Guildenstern in the *Hamlet* plot leading to their deaths. Coin tossing in the opening scene defines the difference between the universe of Shakespeare's Hamlet and the one Stoppard's Rosencrantz and Guildenstern struggle to understand. The image suggests a world in which causality is absent, and presents the notion that a sequence of eighty-five consecutive heads is both surprising and unexpected.

> *Guil*:   It must be indicative of something besides the redistribution of wealth. (*He muses.*) List of possible explanations. One: I'm willing it. Inside where nothing shows, I am the essence of a man spinning double-headed coins, and betting heads against himself in private atonement of unremembered past. (*He spins a coin at Ros.*)

> *Ros*:   Heads.

> *Guil*:   Two: time has stopped dead, and the single experience of one coin being spun once has been repeated ninety times ... (*He flips a coin, looks at it, tosses it to Ros.*) On the whole, doubtful. Three: divine intervention, that is to say, a good turn from above concerning him ... Four: a spectacular vindication of the principle that each individual coin spun

individually (*he spins one*) is as likely to come down heads as tails and therefore should cause no surprise each individual time it does.[12]

The final explanation is statistically accurate and presents us with a world of complete unreliability. The eighty-sixth spin is totally undetermined by the previous eighty-five. Facts remain isolated and all explanations remain equally possible since we cannot comprehend the nature of the circumstances determining the run. Guildenstern himself specifically draws the comparison between the two kinds of world.

Guil: The equanimity of your average tosser of coins depends upon the law, or rather a tendency, or let us say a probability, or at any rate a mathematically calculable chance, which ensures that he will not upset himself by losing too much nor upset his opponent by winning too often. This made for a kind of harmony and a kind of confidence. It related the fortuitous and the ordained into a reassuring union which we recognized as nature. The sun came up about as often as it went down, in the long run, and a coin showed heads about as often as it showed tails. Then a messenger arrived. We had been sent for. Nothing else happened.[13]

The messenger summons them from the endless cycle of fortuitous repetitive facts to a world that proceeds in an ordained linear pattern toward a predetermined end. The summons and the coin tossing, both with each other and with the players, lead to Rosencrantz and Guildenstern being caught in the *Hamlet* pattern.

If the intricate game of coin tossing in the first act introduces the influence of probability and chance over man's life, then the box and the boat serve as appropriate metaphors that illustrate the limited control man has over his own fate. The box has boundaries, and the boat is merely a larger box whose movement on a particular course toward a specific destination has been predetermined. While a passenger is free to move about, speak, and think, he cannot fundamentally alter the course of the vessel. Similarly, man follows a predetermined course starting at birth and moving invariably toward death. Stoppard uses the box and boat metaphors to show how man's ultimate mortality remains an immutable fact despite his freedom to act however he wishes during that span of travel. In Act 2, Rosencrantz recognizes man's mortality and clearly prefers existing within boundaries to not living at all.

> *Ros*: Stuffed in a box like that, I mean you'd be in there for ever. Even taking into account the fact that you're dead, really … *ask* yourself, if I asked you straight off—I'm going to stuff you in this box now, would you rather be alive or dead? Naturally, you'd prefer to be alive. Life in a box is better than no life at all.[14]

Like Rosencrantz, who seems to enjoy the confines of the box, in Act 3, Guildenstern enjoys the contained quality of the boat, which becomes a coffin image.

Guil: Yes, I'm very fond of *boats* myself. I like the way they're contained. You don't have to worry about which way to go, or whether to go at all—the question doesn't arise, because you're on a *boat*, aren't you?[15]

Rosencrantz and Guildenstern's recognition of their destiny should alter the way we respond to them; if they have to die, then so do we. The entire thrust of Stoppard's strategy has been to make us recognize that in our shadow world, the identity of man is defined only by his mortality.

To sum up: In Bloom's terms, Stoppard's vision may seem to be less original than that of Bond because Stoppard does not try to create a movement of discontinuity with Shakespeare by formulating a distinctive antithetical statement. Nevertheless, in the new textual encounter *Rosencrantz and Guildenstern Are Dead*, Stoppard still manages to be the dominant interpreter. By bringing Rosencrantz and Guildenstern and the players to the foreground of his play, and by thoroughly developing his sophisticated use of mirror technique (the play within the play and mimetic scenes), Stoppard establishes his own individual presence.

CONCLUSION

There Will Always Be Eagles

To formulate the theoretical perspective with which we can define the relationship between Shakespeare's original plays and Bond and Stoppard's new versions, we have closely examined Bloom's theory of the anxiety of influence in relation to the concepts of his precursors, W. Jackson Bate and T. S. Eliot. We have considered, modified, and reconstructed the theory of influence to adopt it to the needs of dramatic criticism.

According to the theoretical perspective of this research, a dramatist's version may be judged as original as his precursor's original if the dramatist can swerve away from his precursor by executing a corrective movement in his own play. In the truly new play, the playwright creates a movement of discontinuity with the parent play through an antithetical process.

In the new textual encounter *Lear*, Bond's attempt to be the dominant interpreter is quite evident. The basic difference between Shakespeare's original and Bond's version consists of bond's concern not only with the personal tragedy of the characters, but also for the tragedy of a society that revels in moralized and institutionalized patterns of aggression. Bond believes that Shakespeare's design in *King Lear* is a total arraignment of conventional authority and the morality used to validate and execute it. Bond's urge to reinforce his antithetical statement compels him to drastically change the character relationships as given in Shakespeare's play. Furthermore, Bond ignores the entire Gloucester subplot and embeds the thesis of *King Lear* in the dramatic structure of his own play. Bond's antithetical statement is intensified by his one-sided structure, his development of scenes, and his use of appropriate theatrical imagery.

Despite the apparent derivativeness recognized in *Rosencrantz and Guildenstern Are Dead*, Stoppard established his own individual presence in his new textual encounter. According to the theoretical perspective of this study, Stoppard's version could be judged less original than that of Bond because Stoppard's play lacks a distinctive antithetical statement. In contrast to Bond, Stoppard does not alter the plot or relationships as set in his precursor's text.

Nevertheless, by bringing Rosencrantz and Guildenstern and the players to the foreground of his play and by thoroughly developing his sophisticated use of mirror technique (the play within a play and mimetic scenes), Stoppard accomplishes a brilliant inversion of Shakespeare's material. In the story of two marginal characters in *Hamlet*, Stoppard saw a situation that truly mirrors the absurdity of the human condition. The inevitability of the *Hamlet* plot is deliberately used by Stoppard as a device for denying choice in human affairs. Stoppard retains Shakespeare's terms only to assert his major theme, which is the absurdity of the human condition.

Like Bond, Stoppard uses theatrical imagery basic to the concern, form, and structure of the play.

Despite the differences between the two new versions, both playwrights engage in creative dialogue with the originals, from which arise theatrical experiences of impressive power. Bate believes that there is nothing "approaching or analogous" to Shakespeare's originals, and Keats could not fulfill his hopes of writing fine plays and kept desperately wondering, "why should we be owls … when we can be eagles?" But with this research, by concretely defining the relationships between the new plays and their Shakespearean originals, I would argue that I have demonstrated that both Bond and Stoppard wrote plays that do not suffer in comparison with Shakespeare's great originals. Indeed, these two contemporary playwrights prove that creating new versions analogous to the originals is possible. There will always be eagles.

Endnotes

Introduction:

1. Quoted by W. Jackson Bate in *The Burden of the Past and the English Poet* (Cambridge, Mass. : Harvard Univ. Press, 1970), p.77.

2. C. W. E. Bigsby, *Tom Stoppard* (London: Longman Group Ltd., 1986), p. 4.

3. Leslie Smith, "Edward Bond's *Lear*," *Comparative Drama* 13 (Spring, 1979), p. 72.

4. Ibid., p. 65.

5. Ibid., p. 65.

6. Ibid., p. 68.

7. Ibid., p. 84.

8. Bigsby, *Tom Stoppard*, p. 19.

9. Jill L. Levenson, "'Hamlet' Andante/ 'Hamlet' Allegro: Tom Stoppard's Two Versions," *Shakespeare Survey : An Annual Survey of Shakespearian Study and Production*, 36, (1983), ed. by Stanley Wells, p.21.

10. Ibid., p. 21.

11. Ibid., p. 21.

12. M. H. Abrams. *A Glossary of Literary Terms* (New York: Holt, Holt, Rinehart and Winston, 1981), p. 83.

CHAPTER ONE

1. W. Jackson Bate, *The Burden of the Past and the English Poet* (Cambridge, Mass.; Harvard Univ. Press, 1970), pp. 3-4.

2. Ibid., p. 4.

3. Longinus, "On The Sublime," in *Criticism* H *Twenty Major Statements* ed by Charles Kaplan (Scranton, Pennsylvania: Chandler Publishing Company, 1963), p. 99.

4. Bate, *Burden*, pp. 61, 71.

5. Robert Moynihan, *A Recent Imagining: Interviews with Harold Bloom, Geoffrey Hartman, J. Hillis Miller,*

and Paul de Man (Hamden, Connecticut: the Shoe String Press, 1986), p. 22.

6. Bate *Burden*, p. 31.

7. Ibid., p. 26.

8. Ibid., p. 44.

9. Ibid., p. 6.

10. Ibid., p. 77.

11. Ibid., p. 89.

12. Ibid., p. 56.

13. Ibid., p. 111.

14. Ibid., p. 105.

15. Ibid., p. 106.

16. Ibid., p. 132.

17. Ibid., p. 132.

18. Ibid., p. 106.

19. Ibid., p. 133.

20. *A Recent Imagining*, p. 26.

21. Abrams, *A Glossary*, p. 82.

22. T. S. Eliot, *Selected Essays*: 1917-1932 (New York: Harcourt, Brace and Company, 1932), p.4.

23. Ibid., p. 4.

24. Ibid., p. 4.

25. Ibid., p. 4.

26. Ibid., p. 4.

27. Ibid., p. 5.

28. Harold Bloom, *The Anxiety of Influence: A Theory of Poetry* (New York: Oxford Univ. Press, 1973), p. 37.

29. Eliot, *Selected Essays*, pp. 4-5.

30. Ibid., p. 9.

31. Ibid., p. 4.

32. Lewis Freed, *T. S. Eliot: Aesthetics and History* (La Salle, Illinois: Open Court, 1962), p. 130.

33. Ibid., p. 139.

34. Ibid., p. 139.

35. Ibid., p. 140.

36. Richard Shusterman, *T. S. Eliot and the Philosophy of Criticism* (New York: Columbia Univ. Press, 1988), p. 158.

37. T. S. Eliot *The Use of Poetry and the Use of Criticism: Studies in the Relation of Criticism to Poetry in England* (London: Faber and Faber, Ltd., 1933), p. 35.

38. T. S. Eliot, *On Poetry and Poets* (New York: Fararr, Straus and Cudahy, 1957), p. 171.

39. Bloom, *Anxiety*, p. 11.

40. Bate, Burden, p. 78.

41. Ibid., p. 78.

42. Ibid., p. 78.

43. Ibid., p. 125.

44. Ibid., p. 79.

45. Ibid., p. 97.

46. Ibid., p. 97.

47. Ibid., p. 98.

48. Harold Bloom, *A Map of Misreading* (New York: Oxford Univ. Press, 1975), p. 51.

49. Ibid., p. 59.

50. Ibid., p. 59.

51. Ibid., p. 51.

52. Bloom, *Anxiety*, p. 30.

CHAPTER TWO

1. Quoted by Malcolm Hay and Philip Roberts in *Bond: A Study of His Plays* (London: Eyre Methuen, 1980), p. 105.

2. Ibid., p. 107.

3. Joseph E. Duncan, "The Child and the Old Man in the Plays of Edward Bond" *Modern Drama* 19 (1976) p. 1.

4. Quoted by Leslie Smith in "Edward Bond's *Lear*," *p. 79.*

5. Quoted by Hay and Roberts, p. 105.

6. Ibid., pp. 105-106.

7. Quoted by Leslie Smith in Edward Bond's *Lear*," p. 68.

8. Ibid., p. 83.

9. Quoted by Hay and Roberts, p. 109.

10. Ibid., p. 114.

11. Edward Bond, *Lear* (London: Eyre Methuen Ltd. 1980), p. V.

12. Ibid., p. vii.

13. Ibid., p. vii.

14. Ibid., p. xiii.

15. Ibid., pp. 59-60.

16. Edward bond and Christopher Innes "Edward Bond: From Rationalism to Rhapsody," *Canadian Theatre Review,* 23 (Summer 1979), 112.

17. Christopher Innes, "The Political Spectrum of Edward Bond: From Rationalism to Rhapsody" *Modern Drama* 25, 2 (June, 1982), 189.

18. Peter Brook, *The Empty Space* (New York: Pelican, 1973), p. 152.

19. Quoted by Hay and Roberts, pp. 107-108.

CHAPTER THREE

1. Bond, *Lear*, p. xiv.

2. Horst Oppel and Sandra Christenson, *Edward Bond's Lear and Shakespeare's Lear* (Mainz: Akademie der Wissenschaften und der Literatur, 1973), p. 14.

3. Ibid., p. 14.

4. Ibid., p. 14.

5. Bond, *Lear*, pp. 3-à

6. Bond *Lear*, p. 7.

7. Edward Bond, "An Interview with Tony Coult," *Plays and Players* (December, 1975), p. 13.

8. Bond, *Lear*, p. 9.

9. Leslie Smith, "Edward Bond's *Lear*, p. 75.

10. Ibid., p. 74.

11. Bond, *Lear*, pp. 10-11.

12. Ibid., p. 14.

13. Hay and Roberts, *bond: A Study of His Plays*, p. 117.

14. Bond, *Lear*, p. 26.

15. Quoted by Leslie Smith in "Edward Bond's *Lear*," p. 77.

16. Bond, *Lear*, pp. 34-35.

17. Hay and Roberts, *Bond: A Study of His Plays*, p. 127.

18. Bond, *Lear*, p. 35.

19. Hay and Roberts, *Bond: A Study of His Plays*, p. 127.

20. Bond, *Lear*, p. 41.

21. Bond, *Lear*, p. 42.

22. Quoted by Hay and Roberts in *Bond: A Study of His Plays*, p. 129.

23. Ibid., p. 131.

24. Bond, *Lear*, p: 69.

25. Ibid., p. 66.

26. Ibid., pp. 84-85.

27. Leslie smith, "Edward Bond's *Lear*," p. 66.

28. Ibid., p. 73.

29. Ibid., p. 73.

30. *Lear.* p. 86.

31. Ibid., p. 86.

32. Ibid., p 86.

Chapter Four

1. Ruby Cohn, *Modern Shakespeare Offshoots* (Princeton: Univ. Press, 1976), p. 217; Charles Marowitz, ('Confessions of a counterfeit critic," cited by Christian W. Thomson, "tom Stoppard, *Rosencrantz and Guildenstern Are Dead*: Spiel vom Sterben, Spiel vom Tod, Spiel vom Tod in Leben," in *Maske und Kothurn*, 24 (1978), 124; Thomas Whitaker, *Fields of Play in Modern Drama* (Princeton: Princeton Univ. Press, 1977), p. 14.

2. Quoted by Jill L. Levenson in "'Hamlet' Andante/'Hamlet' Allegro: Tom Stoppard's Two Versions," *Shakespeare Survey: An Annual Survey of Shakespearian study and Production*, 36 (1983), ed. By Stanley ells, p. 22.

3. Ibid., p. 22.

4. Ibid., p. 23.

5. William Babula, "The Play-life Metaphor in Shakespeare and Stoppard," *Modern Drama* 15 (1972), 279.

6. Ronald Hayman, *Tom Stoppard* (London: Heinmann, 1982) p. 46.

7. Quoted by Jill L. Levenson in "'Hamlet' Andante/'Hamlet' Allegro," p. 22.

8. Quoted by Jill L. Levenson in "Views from a revolving door: Tom Stoppard's canon to date," *Queen's Q.* 78 (1971), 435.

9. Paul s. Conklin, *A History of Hamlet Criticism* (New York: The Humanities Press Inc., 1957), p. 1.

10. Claude C. H. Williamson, *Readings on the Character of Hamlet* (London: George Allen and Unwin Ltd., 1953), p. v.

11. Ibid., p. v.

CHAPTER FIVE

1. Ibid., p. 49.

2. Ibid., p. 19.

3. Ibid., p. 57.

4. Ibid., p. 49.

5. Ibid., p. 62.

6. *Hamlet*, p. 111.

7. *Rosencrantz and Guildenstern Are Dead*, p. 25.

8. Ibid., p. 83.

9. Ibid., p. 93.

10. Ibid., p. 50.

11. Ibid., pp. 10-11.

12. Ibid., pp. 12-13.

13. Ibid., p. 75.

14. Ibid., p. 75.

Bibliography

PART ONE: THEORY

Abrams, M. H. *A Glossary of Literary Terms*. New York: Holt, Rinehart and Winston, 1981.

Bate, W. Jackson, *The Burden of the Past and the English Poet*. Cambridge, Mass.: Harvard Univ. Press, 1970.

Bloom, Harold. *Agon: Towards a Theory if Revision. New York*: Oxford Univ. Press, 1982.

_____. *The Anxiety of Influence: A Theory of Poetry*. New York: Oxford Univ. Press, 1973.

_____. *The Breaking of Vessels*. Chicago: Chicago Univ. Press, 1982.

_____. *Figures of Capable Imagination*. New York: Seabury, 1976.

_____. *A Map of Misreading.* New York: Oxford Univ. Press, 1975.

_____. *The Visionary Company: A Reading of English Romantic Poetry.* New York: Doubleday, 1961.

Bruss, Elizabeth W. *Beautiful Theories: The Spectacle of Discourse in Contemporary Criticism.* Baltimore: Johns Hopkins Press, 1982.

Burke, Kenneth. "Father and Son." *New Republic,* 12 Ap. 1975, p. 23-24.

Culler, Jonathan. "Frontiers of Criticism." *Yale Review,* 61 (1971-72), 259-71.

_____. "Reading and Misreading." *Yale Review,* 65 (1975), 88-95.

Derrida, Jacques. *Of Grammatology,* trans. Gaytri Spivak. Baltimore: Johns Hopkins Press, 1976.

_____. *Writing and Difference,* trans. Alan Bass. Chicago: Chicago Univ. Press, 1978.

Donoghe, Denis, "Deconstructing Deconstruction," *New York Review of Books,* 12 June 1980, pp. 37-41.

Eliot, T. S. *Selected Essays: 1971-1932.* New York: Harcourt, Brace and Company. Inc., 1932.

_____. *The Use of Poetry and the Use of Criticism: Studies in the Relation of Criticism to Poetry in England.* London: Faber and Faber Ltd., 1933.

_____. *On Poetry and Poets*. New York Fararr, Straus and Cudahy, 1957.

Freed, Lewis. *L. S. Eliot: Aesthetics and History*. La Salle, Illinois: Open Court, 1962.

Godzich, Wald. "Harold Bloom as Rhetorician." *Centrum, 7*, no. 1 (1978, 43-499

Handleman, Susan A. *The Slayers of Moses: The Emergence of Rabbinic Interpretation in Modern Literary Theory. Albanic Interpretation in Modern Literary Theory.*

Albany State Univ. of New York Press, 1982.

Longinus "On The Sublime," *Criticism: Twenty Major Statements.* Ed. By Charles Kaplan, Scranton, Pennsylvania: Chandler Publishing Company, 1964. pp. 52-90.

Moyniham, Roberts. *A Recent Imagining: Interviews with Harold Bloom, Geoffrey Hartman, J. Hillis Miller, and Paul de Man.* Hamden, Connecticut: The Shoe String Press, 1986.

Shusterman, Richard. *T. S. Eliot and the Philosophy of Criticism.* New York: Columbia Univ. Press, 1988.

PART TWO
THE PLAYRIGHTS
EDWARD BOND

(1) *PLAYS*

The Pope's Wedding. London: Eyre Methuen, 1971.

Saved. London: Eyre Methuen, 1966.

Early Morning. London: Calder and Boyars, 1968.

Narrow Road to the Deep North h A comedy. London: Eyre Methuen, 1968.

Black Mass, Gambit, 5, 17 Oct., 1970.

Lear. London: Eyre Methuen, 1972. (with author's Preface).

The Sea: A Comedy. London: Eyre Methuen, 1973.

Bingo: Scenes of Money and Death. London Eyre Methuen, 1976.

The Fool: Scenes of Bread and Love. London: Eyre Methuen, 1976.

A. A. America! (Grandma Faust: A burlesque and The Swing: A Documentary) London: Eyre Methuen, 1976.

The Bundle: Scenes of Right and Evil or New Narrow Road to the Deep North, London: Eyre Methuen, 1978.

The Woman. London Eyre Methuen, 1978.

(II) SECONDARY SOURCES

Duncan, Joseph E. "The Child and the Old Man in the Plays of Edward Bond," *Modern Drama* 19 (1876) pp. 1-10

Hay, Malcolm, and Philip Roberts, *Bond: A Study of His* Plays, London: Eyre Methuen, 1980.

Innes, Christopher. "The Political Spectrum of Edward Bond: from Rationalism to Rhapsody," *Modern Drama* XXV, 2 (June, 1982), p. 189-206.

Oppel, Horst, and Sanira Christenson, *Edward Bond's Lear and Shakespeare's King Lear.* Mainz: Akademie der Wissenchaften und der Literatur, 1974.

Smith, Leslie. "Edward Bond's *Lear,*" *Comparative Drama* 13 (Spring, 1979), pp. 65-84.

Tom Stoppard

(I) *PLAYS*

Albert Bridge. London: Faber and Faber, 1970.

Artist Descending a Staircase, and Where Are They Now? Two plays for Radio. London: Faber and Faber, 1978

Enter A Free Man. London: Faber and Faber, 1986.

Rosencrantz and Guillenstern Are Dead. London Faber and Faber, 1967.

Travesties. New York: Grove Press, 1975.

Undiscovered Country. Das Weite Land in an English Version by Tom Stoppard, London: Faber and Faber, 1980.

(II) *Secondary Sources*

Babula, W. "The Play-Life Metaphor in Shakespeare and Stoppard," *Modern Drama* 15 (December 1972), 279-81.

Cohn, Ruby. *Modern Shakespeare Offshoots*, Princeton: Princeton Univ. Press, 1976.

Hayman, Ronald. *Tom Stoppard*. Lonlon: Heinmann, 1982.

Levenson, Jill L. "'Hamlet' Andante/'Hamlet' Allegro: Tom Stoppard's Two Versions," *Shakespeare Survey: An Annual Survey of Shakespearian Study and Production* 36 (1983), pp. 21-28.

_____. "Views from a Revolving door: Tom Stoppard's Canon to Date," *Queen's Q.* 78. (1871), pp. 431-442.

WILLIAM SHAKESPEARE

(I)

King Lear London: Longman, 1974.

Hamlet. London: Longman, 1968.

(II) *SECONDARY SOURCES:*

Conklin, Paul S. *A History of Hamlet criticism.* New York: The Humanities Press Inc. 1964.

Frye, Ronald Muskat. *Shakespeare: The Art of The Drama-list.* Boston and New York. Houghton Mifflin Company, 1970.

Gottschalk, Paul. *The Meaning of Hamlet: Modes of Literary Interpretation since Bradley.* Albuquerque Univ. of New Mexico Press. 1972.

_____. "The Universe of Madness in *King Lear.*" *Bucknell Review*, 19 (1971), 51-68.

Herz, Judith Scherer, "Play World and Real world: Dramatic Illusion and The Dream Metaphor," *English Studies in Canada* (Toronto), 3 (1977), 386-400.

McLaughlin, John J. "The Dynamics of Power in *King Lear*: An Alderian Interpretation." *Shakespeare Quarterly*, 29 (1978), 37-43.

Williamson, Claude C.W. *Readings on the Character of Hamlet.* London: George Allen and Unwin Ltd., 1950.